Best Friends

DEVELOPING AN INTIMATE RELATIONSHIP WITH GOD

ARCHIE PARRISH & JOHN PARRISH

WORD BOOKS
PUBLISHER
WACO, TEXAS

A DIVISION OF
WORD, INCORPORATED

Paperback version published by Word, Incorporated, Waco, Texas 76702-2518. Original hardback version published in Nashville, Tennessee, by Oliver-Nelson Books, a division of Thomas Nelson, Inc., Publishers, and distributed in Canada by Lawson Falle, Ltd., Cambridge, Ontario.

Unless otherwise noted, the Bible version used in this publication is the NEW KING JAMES VERSION. Copyright © 1979, 1980, 1982, Thomas Nelson, Inc., Publishers. Used by permission of Thomas Nelson, Inc., Publishers.

Scripture quotations noted NEB are from *The New English Bible.* © The Delegates of the Oxford University Press and the Syndics of the Cambridge University Press 1961, 1970. Reprinted by permission.

Scripture quotations noted NIV are from *The Holy Bible: New International Version.* Copyright © 1978 by the New York International Bible Society. Used by permission of Zondervan Bible Publishers.

Scripture quotations noted NASB are from the *New American Standard Bible,* © The Lockman Foundation 1960, 1962, 1963, 1968, 1971, 1972, 1973, 1975, 1977, and are used by permission.

Scripture quotations noted TEV are from the *Good News Bible* New Testament. Copyright © American Bible Society 1966, 1971, 1976. Used by permission.

Scripture quotations noted TLB are from *The Living Bible* (Wheaton, Illinois: Tyndale House Publishers, 1971) and are used by permission.

Library of Congress Cataloging-in-Publication Data
Parrish, Archie, 1932-
    Best friends.
    1. God—Worship and love. 2. Christian life—
1960-   I. Parrish, John, 1955-
II. Title.
BV4817.P37 1987   248.4   87-29596
ISBN 0-8499-3112-6

898 B A   98765432

Printed in the United States of America.

Best Friends
is
dedicated to
Jesus of Nazareth,
our
God,
Savior,
and
Best Friend

There is a friend who
sticks closer than
a brother.

Proverbs 18:24

He made me into a polished arrow
and concealed me in his quiver.

Isaiah 49:2 NIV

Contents

Acknowledgments

$\mathcal{S}$pecial thanks go to the following friends who have helped to make this book a reality.

Family: To Jean, Jane, Anne, Fred, Cyrus, Phyllis, and Jesse—friends for a lifetime from God and our most enthusiastic encouragers through this venture.

Serve International Staff: Robert Beavin, Richard Colyer, Beverly Doty, Fred Fisher, Lorey Gilmer, Chris Lassen, Debbie Liss, Susan Pannell, Jean Parrish, Sheryl Toph, Pat Walden, Wanza Walston, and Rich Wedekind.

Serve International Board of Directors: Tom Bush, Kenneth Carter, David Grubbs, Terry Gyger, Richard Hostetter, David Howard, Harvey Milkon, and R. C. Sproul.

Friends: Lee Armfield, Gail Berg, Bobb and Cheryl Biehl, Ezra and Lois Clemens, Dora Hillman, C. Buck and Ruth LeCraw, Bob Legler, Hugh Maclellan, Sr., Lois, Lisa and Lara Mowday, Al and Patsy Rhodes, Rick and Barbara Saul, C. Peter Wagner, and C. Davis Weyerhaeuser.

Field Test Groups: Rev. Bob Catlin and Denny Shantz, Trinity Presbyterian Church, Clearwater, Florida; Rev. C. G. Ingram and Rev. George Dainty, Northside Alliance Church,

9

Best Friends

Atlanta, Georgia; Rev. Rich Plass, Peace Community Church, Frankfort, Illinois; Rev. Walter Sandell, Rev. Al Bosenberg, Ron Mitchell, Peter Wallace, Lewis Von Herman, and Diane Lewis, First Alliance Church, Atlanta, Georgia; Rev. Dave Owens and Vicki Hendrickson, Millard Community Church, Omaha, Nebraska; and Mrs. Lois Mowday, Covenant Presbyterian Church, Colorado Springs, Colorado.

Many others have contributed to this book whose names we cannot list due to space but who are no less special to us. To these, we also extend our gratitude.

Introduction:
Pegs of Truth

*B*ecoming the kind of person who can have an intimate relationship with God may be compared to the ancient process of making a straight shaft for an arrow from a rough, crooked branch.

The craftsman began the process by selecting the proper wood. He stripped the branch of all leaves and twigs and then thrust it into the flames of the fire.

Carefully he eyed the branch, pulling it out the moment before the fire would kindle it. The heat made the branch pliable.

Next to the fire, the craftsman would drive two rows of pegs into the ground in a straight line, an inch or less apart. As the crooked branch was pulled from the fire, it was immediately forced between the pegs.

After the branch cooled, the craftsman would take it out. He placed it back into the flames, and once again he withdrew the branch and forced it between the pegs, but on a different plane. Crooked places not caught on the first shaping were then straightened.

The craftsman repeated the process until he was satisfied. Then with a sharp knife, he removed all the charred bark. Next, he took sand and a bit of old animal skin and polished the shaft until it was so smooth that his bare hand could detect no roughage. As a final touch, he rubbed oil into the shaft until it shone in the sunlight. The crooked, unpromising piece of wood had become a thing of beauty.

Feathers were attached to one end of the shaft and a sharp tip was attached to the other end. The feathers caused the arrow to fly straight to its target, and the tip enabled it to penetrate.

As in the natural, so it is in the spiritual. Scripture states, "He made me into a polished arrow and concealed me in his quiver" (Isaiah 49:2 NIV). An imperfect person is like a crooked branch, but any person who trusts Jesus Christ as Savior, Lord, and Best Friend has the potential to become a polished arrow special to God. But better than the inanimate arrow, a Christian can develop an intimate, living relationship with God. Through the ministry of the Holy Spirit, the imperfect believer is made pliable, just as the green branch is affected by the fire. Thirteen basic biblical truths can serve as pegs to guide a Christian in a growing relationship with God just as the craftsman's pegs guide a crooked stick into a straight arrow. As your life is lined up between these pegs, the crooked places that harm an intimate awareness of God are made straight. As this refining process is repeated, your relationship with God grows more and more intimate.

The thirteen chapters of this book explain the pegs of truth that the Holy Spirit uses to straighten and strengthen your life so that you can develop a more intimate relationship with God and an increased awareness of His presence with you.

PART I | *Evaluating Your Friendship with God*

1

Closer Than a Brother

1   Proper Intimacy

*F*or nearly ten years, Larry and Stan's friendship was tested in many ways. But they admired and respected one another, even when they strongly disagreed on the way a job should be done.

When tragedy struck in Larry's family, Stan laid aside everything else he was doing to be by his friend's side. For Stan, the most important thing was to make sure Larry knew that he could always depend on him.

When the work that Stan had poured his life into for thirteen years seemed to crumble around him, Larry seemed to know instinctively that life was pressing Stan to the breaking point. He would call or drop by, and he always had the right word for the moment. Because of Larry's support, Stan pulled his life back together and moved on to bigger and better dreams.

When Stan's work required that he move a thousand miles away, there were fewer opportunities for the two to express their friendship, but they were still there. Stan knew that if tragedy struck in his life, Larry would lay aside anything he was doing and stand with him for as long as was necessary.

The person who experiences this kind of friendship is rich indeed. But every human friendship has its limitations. Human beings can only do so much. But there is one person who does not have these limitations.

Many of us have experienced a friendship we thought would last forever. Sometimes the slightest incident can shatter a relationship we thought would never end.

What would you call a person who
- Knows everything about you—all your faults and shortcomings—and still loves you all the time?
- Accepts you as you are but will not let you settle for being anything less than everything you can possibly be?
- Is so close you feel as though the two of you have one soul?
- Wants you to be totally honest and open with him all the time?
- Has experienced every kind of trial you will ever face and has overcome each one and is eager to help you become an overcomer also?
- Freely chooses to commit himself to you and is willing to work at developing the relationship by the process of mutual giving in ever-increasing degrees in the new experiences of life?
- Sticks closer than a brother?
- Is willing to lay down his life for you?

I would call Him "friend, my very best friend!"

Only one person in the world is this kind of friend.

His name is Jesus. Let's consider what friendship with Jesus means.

Close Friends in the Bible

Some people say they have dozens of friends but no one is really close to them. A few close friends add depth to life we can never have with many shallow relationships.

Ruth and Naomi were close friends. Naomi's husband died. Ruth married one of Naomi's sons, but he died too. In this tragic situation, Ruth said to Naomi, "Wherever you go, I will go; and wherever you lodge, I will lodge; your people shall be my people, and your God, my God. Where you die, I will die, and there will I be buried. The LORD do so to me, and more also, if anything but death parts you and me" (Ruth 1:16–17).

Jonathan and David were close friends. Jonathan was the son of Saul, the first king of Israel. David was the shepherd boy chosen by the Lord to become king after Saul—a position that should have been filled by Jonathan. But "the soul of Jonathan was knit to the soul of David, and Jonathan loved him as his own soul" (1 Samuel 18:1).

These are two examples of close friendships in the Bible, but there is another one that is even more significant.

During the three years of Jesus' earthly ministry before He was crucified, John was His closest friend. Though Jesus cared for all His disciples, only John refers to himself as "the disciple whom Jesus loved" (John 20:2; 21:20). He was at the cross when Jesus died, and it was to John that Jesus entrusted the care of Mary, His mother (see John 19:26–27).

After Jesus came out of the grave alive and returned

to heaven, John lived another sixty years. During this time, he continued to grow in his close, intimate relationship with Jesus.

In the early Church the symbol for the apostle John was an eagle. An ancient legend says the eagle is the only creature on earth that can soar into the sun and look at it with the naked eye without going blind. John "soared" closer to the Son of God than anyone else, and he tells us things about Jesus that no one else knew. Through John we learn that Jesus is our Friend and we learn how that friendship will express itself.

Jesus as Your Close Friend

When you truly rely on Jesus Christ alone for your eternal life, a new relationship is established. Jesus becomes your personal Savior and Lord. You become a member of God's family. Jesus becomes your Friend—your very Best Friend. In New Testament days, calling someone "friend" meant regarding the individual with as much love and commitment as that given a close relative. When you become a friend of Jesus, it is as if you have become a relative of Jesus. And, most amazing of all, He wants you to be His friend!

Jesus once said, "Greater love has no one than this, than to lay down one's life for his friends" (John 15:13). Then He laid down His life! He is the Friend who loves at all times (see Proverbs 17:17). He is the Friend who sticks closer than a brother (see Proverbs 18:24).

Jesus is not just a great man from past history. He is the "one Mediator between God and men" (1 Timothy 2:5). He is the *only* person who is both true God and true man. He is the *only* person who ever lived a perfect, sinless life. As the sinless God-man, He was the *only* one able to pay the penalty for sin by His death on the cross. He is the *only* religious leader in all history to prove He is God by coming out of the grave alive.

Abraham was the father of God's ancient people, Israel. The highest compliment ever given him was to be called God's friend (see James 2:23).

Jesus said, "I and My Father are one" (John 10:30). And because of this truth, you will note a deliberate interchange of *God* and *Jesus* throughout this book. The purpose is not to confuse you but to impress the fact that Jesus is God. Friendship with Jesus is friendship with the one true God! You too can be God's friend.

To be God's friend first and foremost means being properly related to God the Son. The relationship of the earth to the sun is a good illustration. The earth orbits around the sun at exactly the right distance for life to survive and thrive. If the earth were closer, life would incinerate. If it were farther away, life would freeze. In similar fashion, the friends of God have a proper place to fill in relation to God the Son. The proper place is one of reverent intimacy.

Intimacy without proper reverence will result in certain judgment (see 2 Chronicles 26:16–21). Reverence without intimacy results in coldness, an empty, dead, routine ritual. Relate to God with proper respect and intimacy and the joy of your friendship will constantly grow.

Have you ever watched a couple that have been happily married for fifty years? It is uncanny that they can speak so infrequently with each other, yet each can tell what the other may be thinking or feeling at a given moment. Over the years each has gained a familiarity with the other to the extent that they virtually can read the other person's mind without speaking.

Friends, in the deepest sense of the word, are persons who are so close they feel as though they have one soul. This intimacy is similar to the relationship Jesus desires to have with you through His Spirit. He said, "I will pray the Father, and He will give you another Helper, that He may abide forever, even the Spirit of truth,...He dwells with you and will be in you" (John 14:16–17).

Experience of the Intimate Personal Presence of Jesus in Your Life

How intimate and personal is your relationship with God? To some degree this can be determined by how often you sense His presence in your life. Use the intimacy scale to evaluate yourself. Put a check by the number that best describes your awareness of God right now.

Intimacy Scale

	1.	*By the minute*—every waking minute
	2.	*Hourly*—frequently during the day
	3.	*Daily*—some time each day
√	4.	*Weekly*—perhaps associated with religious services
	5.	*Monthly*—occasionally through the year
	6.	*Yearly*—on occasions such as Christmas, Easter or the anniversary of a loved one's death
	7.	*Seldom*—at a crisis, such as a death in the family or a financial reversal

Briefly answer the following questions:

1. What thoughts or questions came to your mind as you evaluated yourself? *Thinking about how there are*
2. Why did you rate yourself as you did? *highs + Low*
3. Are you closer or farther away than you were last week?
4. Where would you like to be on the scale? /

Because thats how we feel right now

Take a few moments before reading further to evaluate some of your friendships, either current or past. *confidentiality,* Why did you consider these people your friends? Why *concern,* were you considered a friend by them? How did you *affirmation,* sustain your intimacy? Where would you put these *keep in touch* friends on the intimacy scale? What is probably differ- *Same* ent and what is similar about your developing friend- *reasons* ship with Jesus? *It takes more than a phone call to be aware of his presence. He* As you consider your relationship with God keep *knows* these thoughts in mind. *me better than any of these friends so I feel sometimes he cant possibly accept me*

stay in touch

The bible tells us he does except us, warts and all. He doesn't leave us in time of crisis.

1. No one seems to stay in a minute-by-minute, continuous awareness of Christ for long periods.
2. If your sense of Jesus' presence is less than daily, you should be concerned about increasing it. Don't be satisfied with less, but don't load yourself with an improper sense of guilt.
3. As long as you live in this world, you will need to grow in your relationship with Jesus. To do this you must desire above all things to have a continuous awareness of Christ's presence in your life.

Let's investigate how God says we can increase our awareness of His presence with us in Chapter 2.

Reflections

1. What do I understand this to be saying? *One should strive for a deeper relationship with Jesus but not despair when it isn't there all the time*

2. What is God telling me to do that I'm not afraid to do?

3. What do I want to understand better?
   God's love & acceptance

4. What is God telling me that I find hard to apply to my life?
   Make time for Him everyday, even when I feel out of touch with Him.

2

Aiming to Please

2   Loving Obedience

*N*ew York's Madison Avenue advertisers have spent millions of dollars on research to learn how to get their products into your mind and to persuade you to purchase their goods. The research, according to *Advertising Age* Magazine, shows that the average person must see or hear the name of the product at least three times before recognizing it. But recognition is not enough. The advertiser must also create a desire for the person to own the product. Recognition and desire are necessary before you will purchase an item.

As you consider the following thoughts about intimacy with God, your mind will be fast at work. Before you own anything in your heart, it must pass through three guards that protect your heart. Each guard tends to be an automatic reaction; you may be unaware of it, yet you experience it. The three guards are

1. *The guard of understanding.* You must understand something to properly respond.

2. *The ethical guard* (what you believe is right and wrong). If you understand something and believe it is right, it will be easier for you to do it. What you understand but believe to be wrong will be difficult for you to do.

God's Word is *always* right. But some of its teachings may be hard for you to apply. When you find a hard saying, don't just pass over it. Make note of it. Pray that God will help you properly respond. Share your concern with a Christian friend and ask him or her to help you.

3. *The emotional guard* (your concern for your well-being). If you understand something and believe it is right but fear that doing it will hurt you more than help you, you will struggle with doing it—or may not even try to do it.

At times you will need to weigh apparent present benefits against actual eternal benefits. Paul put it this way, "The sufferings of this present time are not worthy to be compared with the glory which shall be revealed in us" (Romans 8:18).

Four questions will help you deal with your three guards. Tuck these in your mind and react to the following thoughts about loving obedience in the light of these questions:

1. What do I understand this to be saying? (understanding)
2. What is God telling me to do that I'm not afraid to try? (emotional)
3. What do I want to understand better? (understanding)

4. What is God telling me that I find hard to apply to my life? (ethical or emotional)

Friendship Grows by Loving Obedience

Jesus said, "You are My friends if you do whatever I command you" (John 15:14). He explained, "He who has My commandments and keeps them, it is he who loves Me. And he who loves Me will be loved by My Father, and I will love him and manifest Myself to him" (John 14:21). Friendship with Jesus is expressed by loving obedience. This is not mere doing of duty. It is obedience that flows freely and eagerly from a heart of love.

Lisa may respond to a marriage proposal from Bryan on the basis of love or obligation. If she responds from obligation, she will say to herself, *I don't have any affection for him, but because he has been good to me I owe him a yes.* There is no desire or attraction on her part toward him. However, if Lisa loves Bryan, she will respond to him with a yes that comes with all of her affection and desire. She is drawn to him. Loving obedience is likewise preferable to Jesus. He is pleased when we obey out of love rather than reluctant duty.

Have you ever met Christians who were motivated by "hellfire and brimstone" theology to accept Christ because they were afraid of the alternative? If their understanding is not balanced with the doctrine of God's overwhelming love, they may view the heavenly Father as a tyrant who is ready to strike them down at the slightest mistake. They may obey the Lord, but only because they are afraid of the consequences if they don't. God would much rather we obey His Word because we love Him and want to please Him in all we do as a way of saying thank you. God enables us to love as we should, "because the love of God has been poured out in our hearts by the Holy Spirit who was given to us" (Romans 5:5).

Obedience is not the condition on which Jesus loves you. Instead, loving obedience is the sign that you have received His love. John explained, "We love, because He first loved us" (1 John 4:19 NASB). Jesus' words, lovingly obeyed, cause Him to show more of Himself to you, and the friendship grows.

Loving obedience is the best way you can thank Jesus for all He has done for you. You will need to grow in your friendship with Him, and growth will come when your desire to know Him better exceeds everything else.

Whether you have trusted Jesus as your Savior and Lord for five minutes or fifty years, friendship with Him must be developed by loving obedience. The more consistent your loving obedience is, the more Jesus reveals Himself to you and the more your friendship grows.

Let's take a closer look at this thought. Jesus said, "He who has My commandments and keeps them, it is he who loves Me. And he who loves Me will be loved by My Father, and I will love him and manifest Myself to him" (John 14:21). The words of John encourage us: "Beloved, now we are children of God; and it has not yet been revealed what we shall be, but we know that when He is revealed, we shall be like Him, for we shall see Him as He is" (1 John 3:2).

At this point, one thing must be clarified. You enter the family relationship with God by grace alone, through faith alone, in Christ alone! Once the family relationship exists, then friendship with Jesus grows through loving obedience to His Word. A songwriter expressed it this way:

Trust and obey, for there's no other way
To be happy in Jesus, but to trust and obey.

Once you trust, you will have a growing ability to obey the Lord. You will also have a strong desire to please Him.

Remember, when the Bible speaks, it speaks with authority and truth. "If we confess our sins," the Bible says, "He is faithful and just to forgive us our sins and to cleanse us from all unrighteousness" (1 John 1:9). God cannot lie, and His Truth is good for all eternity. Romans 10:9–10 says if we "confess with [our] mouth the Lord Jesus and believe in [our] heart that God has raised Him from the dead, [we] will be saved." Then we can know that we have been born again. If we have been born again, it also follows that we will love Him. If we love Him, we will want to obey Him. Aim to please Him by lovingly obeying His commands.

The whole Bible is the Word of Christ. As you look through the New Testament, you will notice many words are recorded that Jesus spoke while He was here on earth. Sprinkled throughout His speaking are many commands. Take these commands to heart and seek to make them a part of your thinking. The more you think about them, the more you will be ready to apply them and obey Jesus out of loving obedience.

Growth Spiral

The growth spiral demonstrates the principle of in-

creasing intimacy with Jesus by loving obedience as revealed in John 14:21. The numbers correspond to those
found in the intimacy scale you worked with earlier in
Chapter 1. On the growth spiral the smaller the number the closer a person is to being one with God (see
John 17:20,21). As we grow in intimacy with God, we
grow in oneness with Him.

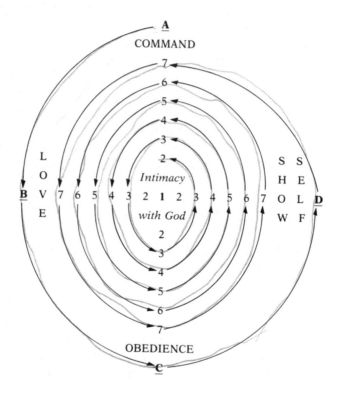

With a pencil, start at Point A. Point A represents the
command of Christ coming to you. If you love Him
(trace with a quarter circle a line from Point A to Point

B) out of a heart that has been redeemed and energized by the Spirit of God, your response to the command of Christ is obedience (trace with a quarter circle a line from Point B to Point C). Loving obedience is rewarded by Christ revealing more of Himself to you (draw a quarter circle from Point C to Point D). As He reveals still more of Himself to you, He gives new commands (draw a quarter circle from Point D to A7) to which you respond with increasing loving obedience. That will again be rewarded with Christ showing more of Himself to you, which brings you to a place where He can give you more commands. (Continue drawing the spiral until it is complete.)

To see how this works, let's consider Bob's experiences. Bob is reading his Bible one day when in Philippians 4:6–7 he sees the command (Point A): "Be anxious for nothing, but in everything by prayer and supplication, with thanksgiving, let your requests be made known to God; and the peace of God, which surpasses all understanding, will guard your hearts and minds through Christ Jesus." Bob realizes that prayer has not been a very consistent part of his friendship with Jesus. Out of love (Point B), Bob decides he will set aside ten minutes every day for prayer. As he does this for a few days (Point C), he gains a greater sense of God's presence and God's concern for his daily affairs (Point D). Bob notices that he has become less anxious as he senses that God hears his requests and will act.

In Bob's prayer time one day, the Lord seems to speak to him through another command he just read from Mark 11:25 (Point A7): "And whenever you stand praying, if you have anything against anyone, forgive him, that your Father in heaven may also forgive you your trespasses." Bob remembers some heated words he had with his neighbor who backed over his trash cans yesterday. The cans were sitting by the road for the day's pickup when the neighbor, who was in a rush to get to work, accidentally hit them. Bob was angry as he ran out to confront his neighbor. As Bob prays and meditates on this command and its implications in this situation, Bob realizes that to obey the Lord here means he must forgive his neighbor (Point B7). When Bob finishes praying, he walks over to his neighbor's. He seeks to mend the relationship, asking for forgiveness for his outburst of anger (Point C7). He explains that their friendship is worth more to him than a couple of garbage cans. Bob then invites his neighbor over for a cookout that Saturday, and the neighbor accepts the invitation. The tension is gone, the relationship is restored.

As Bob walks back to his house, he senses the presence of the Lord with him in a new and closer way (Point D7). He has obeyed the Lord and the Lord has disclosed Himself to Bob in a way that deepens their relationship.

Through this ever-deepening process, your relationship with Jesus grows. You will not leap from seven to one, but you will grow step by step. Scripture calls this the process of growing "in the grace and knowledge of our Lord and Savior Jesus Christ" (2 Peter 3:18). Here the word *knowledge* goes beyond mere intellectual understanding. It means growing in your personal experiences of everyday life.

As we continue on the spiral of experiences and responses leading to new and deeper obedience, we realize what is happening. We are beginning to respond to and be obedient to the Greatest Commandment. How we can continue to grow in relation to this commandment is the subject of Chapter 3.

Reflections

1. What do I understand this to be saying?

   A deeper relationship w/the Lord is a step by step process that begins with our everyday life.

2. What is God telling me to do that I'm not afraid to do? *To forgive others & not dwell on minor disappointments*

3. What do I want to understand better?

   God's forgiveness

4. What is God telling me that I find hard to apply to my life? *To strive to see the good & not the faults in other people.*

PART II | *Strengthening Your Friendship with God*

3
The Key to Intimacy

3   The Greatest Commandment

*F*or months Jane had anticipated her fifteenth birthday so she could begin driving. She had studied eagerly for her learner's permit. Having passed the test, she raced to the car to sit in the driver's seat. As her father climbed into the car with her, he noticed a bewildered look on her face. After staring at the steering wheel, she sheepishly turned to him and asked, "What do I do first?"

With a chuckle he said, "First you place the key in the ignition and turn it away from you to start the car." He knew that he did not have to explain the inner workings of the engine or the electrical and mechanical systems of the car. Since they were in good condition, they would naturally perform their functions if the key was inserted and turned. With the turning of the key, power surged through the car, and Jane was off for her first adventurous drive.

The key to developing an intimate relationship with

God is what is called "the first and greatest commandment" (Matthew 22:39–40). When we take hold of this commandment with the heart, power is released to do everything necessary to be the friend of God.

Let's consider the commandment to which Jesus gave the highest priority. It is our guide for expressing love to God.

As you consider the Greatest Commandment, ask yourself these four brief questions:

1. What do I understand this to be saying? *say things about myself that would I say about other people?*
2. What is God telling me to do that I'm not afraid to try? *Seek to serve God in all persons.*
3. What do I want to understand better?
4. What is God telling me that I find hard to apply to my life? *Focusing on my own issues + not everyone elses.*

Do you want to increase your friendship with Jesus? You can by lovingly obeying His commands. It follows that you need to be aware of what these commands are. They can be found sprinkled throughout the Bible.

However, Jesus called only one command the "greatest" and the "first." For thousands of years people devoted to the Lord have started and ended each day reciting the words of this command as their prayer and declaration of faith. This greatest and first command is:

> You shall love the Lord your God with all your heart, with all your soul, and with all your mind (Matthew 22:37).

Then Jesus added:

> And the second is like it: "You shall love your neighbor as yourself." On these two commandments hang all the Law and the Prophets (Matthew 22:39–40).

Jesus was saying that all of your responsibilities in life can be summed up in these words, "love the Lord your God with all your heart" and "love your neighbor as yourself." If you lovingly obey these commands, then you will have automatically kept all the others.

Since the whole Word of God hangs on these two commandments, you can simplify what you must do to increase your friendship with Jesus by focusing on them. You can show you are Jesus' friend by obeying these key commandments that tell you (1) who you are to love and (2) how you are to love.

1. *Who am I to love?* "You shall love *the Lord your God*...You shall love *your neighbor.*"

2. *How am I to love?* "Love the Lord your God with *all*...Love your neighbor *as yourself.*"

What does it mean to love God with *all your heart*? To answer this you must first understand what your heart is. It consists of your deepest desires, your way of thinking, and your choices.

When we love God with our whole heart, we are choosing to develop a committed, responsible relationship with God. Out of loving obedience we choose to adapt our desires to God's deepest desires. If our thoughts were recorded, they would play back thoughts that are true, pure, and encouraging as we attempt to think more like Jesus thought and spoke. As we love God, our choices will reflect more and more God's choices rather than choices that reflect selfish and self-serving ambitions.

The second command Jesus gave, he compared in importance to the first. What does it mean to "love your neighbor as yourself"? Jesus was saying, "In the manner in which you naturally care for your own well-be-

"LOVE THE LORD YOUR GOD WITH ALL YOUR HEART . . ."

Matthew 22:37

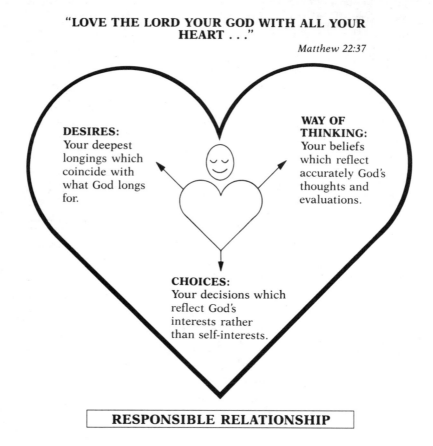

DESIRES:
Your deepest longings which coincide with what God longs for.

WAY OF THINKING:
Your beliefs which reflect accurately God's thoughts and evaluations.

CHOICES:
Your decisions which reflect God's interests rather than self-interests.

RESPONSIBLE RELATIONSHIP

ing, care for others." For example, we make sure we have plenty of the right food to eat. We try to promote our health. We look out for our best interests by nature. To the degree we do this for ourselves, Jesus said we are to do this for others. In Luke 10:29–37 Jesus clarified for us who our neighbor is: Our neighbor is anyone we see in need.

When Jane and Allen Weber moved into a "well-to-do" neighborhood, they soon found out that the families around them had their own friends and were not especially eager to expand their group. Even though they spoke cordially to one another, they recognized the Webers as strangers, and no one offered to get acquainted. The Webers soon adopted the attitude of their neighbors and invited their church friends over occasionally.

A young couple moved into the neighborhood directly across the street from the Webers. Like the rest of the neighbors, the Webers waved cordially but did not attempt to make friends with the new couple. After several weeks had passed, Jane thought about her new neighbor and remembered the loneliness she experienced when she first moved into the area.

Mustering her courage, Jane walked across the street and rang the doorbell of her new neighbor's home. When the young woman answered the door, Jane noticed tears in her eyes.

"Is anything wrong?" Jane asked. "I'm Jane Weber from across the street, and I thought I should get acquainted with you."

"Oh, thank God," the young woman responded. "I am so lonely and depressed, especially since my husband has had to be out of town during the past two weeks. I don't know anybody here, and I don't have anyone to talk to."

Here was a need, and Jane was glad to fill it! The two women became good friends, and together they were able to spark a closeness with other families in the area.

Jesus says if we keep these two commands, to "love the Lord your God with all your heart" and to "love your neighbor as yourself," then we will be showing our love for Him.

Loving God Through Worship

Jesus fleshed out some of the practical implications of the Greatest Commandment. One facet of loving God involves our worship with Him. Friendship with Jesus grows through worship. Jesus said God the Father seeks true worshipers who worship Him in spirit and in truth (John 4:23–24).

Worship is the adoration of God as He is revealed in the Lord Jesus Christ. Love that reaches down from the holy God to sinful man is *grace*. Love that reaches out from one person to another is *affection*. Love that rises up from man to God is *worship*.

To worship God we must be quite conscious of His grace—worship is the overflow of our hearts when we adore Him. As we learn to worship, we learn to be occupied with the Lord.

In a Scandinavian country there is a statue of Christ. A tourist standing in front of it appeared dismayed. A local resident asked what his problem was. He replied, "I cannot see His face." The resident then explained, "If you desire to see His face, you must kneel at His feet."

Worship is the result of seeing and acknowledging

God for who He is. The original meaning of the word *worship* means to "prostrate one's self." As we see God for who He is and experience His presence in our lives, we will desire to respond by worshiping God in humble respect, as the resident of the town knew.

Worship Begins with Me

Worship that pleases God must first be individual. A daily time of reading God's Word, reflecting on it, and talking with God about it gives us power to face the challenges of the day. Private time with the Lord helps us properly develop every other relationship we have. Individual worship is the glue that holds every area of our lives together.

When we set aside a regular time to develop our relationship with the Lord, we are actually fulfilling the command to love God. At the same time, we are also being empowered by God to love ourselves and others more deeply. We begin to see ourselves as we are in relationship to God, and by His grace and love He also shows us how we are becoming more and more like Him. This is one of the many facets of the mystery of worship.

Jesus set the pattern for us. Sometimes He got up before sunrise to spend time with His Father. Sometimes when the work was overwhelming, He would slip off to be alone with the Father.

It is best to have this time alone with God the first thing every day. The time to tune a musical instrument is before the concert. The best time to tune your life with the Lord is before you start your daily activities.

If possible, it is best to have a place free from distractions. Many people like to set aside a special place in their homes for their personal worship of God. This place might be the rocker by the window in your bedroom, a closet that has been emptied, a small writing desk, or a corner of the basement or attic. For others it might be an entire room set aside for their relationship with God.

Personal worship is the primary source of power in your life. The more consistent you are at this point, the more strength you will have to accomplish God's will. As you worship God, you demonstrate your love to Him and fulfill the first and greatest commandment. This pleases God, and He promises to disclose Himself to you more intimately as you obey Him in this specific manner.

In Chapter 4 we'll consider another facet of how to love God with all of our hearts: Reading the Bible.

Reflections

1. What do I understand this to be saying?

   I need to spend more time with God if I want to replenish my spiritual well.

2. What is God telling me to do that I'm not afraid to do? To make time for Him

3. What do I want to understand better?

   Why He becomes least in my life when I need Him most.

4. What is God telling me that I find hard to apply to my life?

   To put my total faith in Him + not worry.

Reading God's Mind

4   Scripture Reading

*H*ow can you grow to know God intimately and personally? The Bible teaches that no one can make himself grow. In Matthew 6:27 Jesus said, "Is there a man of you who by anxious thought can add a foot to his height?" (NEB). While it is true that work and worry cannot force physical growth, there are certain physical laws that, when followed, will ultimately produce growth in a growing body.

At least three specific elements are needed for physical growth: proper food, proper exercise, and proper rest. Just as there are certain elements required to produce physical growth, there are specific elements required to produce spiritual growth. One prerequisite for spiritual growth is a regular intake of God's Word. God tells us, "Like newborn babies crave pure spiritual milk, so that by it you may grow up in your salvation" (1 Peter 2:2 NIV). His Word answers the questions necessary for us to grow.

How can you understand God's desires for your life?

How can you show God you love Him in a tangible way? You can learn the answers as you commit yourself to the daily habit of reading the Bible.

As we explore how reading God's Word can affect our relationship with Him, attempt to evaluate what you read through the filter of four brief questions:

1. What do I understand this to be saying?
2. What is God telling me to do that I'm not afraid to try?
3. What do I want to understand better?
4. What is God telling me that I find hard to apply to my life?

Use these four questions to think through the ideas in this chapter.

As you individually worship the Lord, He wants you to listen to Him. Consider first what He has to say to you before you consider what you want to say to Him. Listening is important in any relationship, and that principle certainly holds true in your relationship with Jesus. The way that you get to know the thoughts of your Friend, Jesus, is through reading His book the Bible. In its pages Jesus speaks. The more you read, the more you will begin to think like He thinks, and the more your mind will share His values and priorities, and the more you will grow spiritually.

The Bible is like no other book in the world. What makes it so unique? God communicates through it. It speaks with divine authority. No other book has the power to convict of sin or to renew an individual and produce a clean life. Alive and powerful, the Bible is sharper than any double-edged sword. It can energize your spirit. It also can cut right to the inner thoughts and motives of your heart (see Hebrews 4:12).

What would you say is the central theme of the Bible? Can you guess what it is? The central theme of the Bible is a person. As you read the printed pages, you will find yourself faced with the person of Jesus. He said, "These are they [the Scriptures] which testify of Me" (John 5:39). As you read the Old Testament, you will find it is continually looking forward to His coming. As you read the New Testament, you will find it says He has come and it tells about the impact of His coming upon our lives.

In those same pages, written hundreds of years before you were born, you are told that your response to Him will be love. You are to love Him with all your mind. Your old self-centered framework of thought will undergo transformation. The apostle Paul said, "Do not be conformed to this world, but be transformed by the renewing of your mind" (Romans 12:2).

Renovating Your Mind

As you read the Bible and are continually faced with your Friend Jesus, your thinking will be renovated (see Colossians 3:8–10). When you were an enemy of Jesus, your thoughts were as an old house showing the effects of years of neglect: boards had rotted through, windows were broken, and paint was peeling. These were the effects of years of sinful, self-centered thinking. As soon as you become Jesus' friend, the house of your mind begins to be renovated. As you read His Word, new boards replace the rotted boards, windows are replaced, and paint is applied in needed spots. Your old thoughts, desires, and choices begin the process of being replaced by a new and better way of thinking. You begin to think like Jesus thinks when you become His friend. You begin to think pure thoughts, loving thoughts, and encouraging thoughts (Philippians 4:8). The way you grow to experience these thoughts and to renovate your mind is through reading His Word. In this way your thought life undergoes a reprogramming process. Your thoughts become more like Jesus' thoughts. This is a lifetime process. You are, as it were, permanently under construction while on this earth.

God promises to help you understand His Word if you are first willing to do what He tells you. He says: "Turn at my reproof; Surely I will pour out my spirit on you; I will make my words known to you" (Proverbs 1:23). His reproof comes with conviction of your sinful attitudes, motives, and deeds as you read His Word. This is the tearing-down process in the renovation of your mind. The Holy Spirit uses God's Word to pry away the old boards and peeling paint of wrong thinking and behavior. He then restores and heals by building you up anew with healing. God's Spirit will help you understand His Word and apply it as you read it.

Where Do You Begin?

The Bible is a library of sixty-six books. All together these books total hundreds of pages. Every Christian should seek to gain an understanding of the whole Bible, which may appear to be a monumental task. No one can do it, however, all at once. How can we expect to master hundreds of pages of writing? No one can eat an elephant in one sitting. But one person can if he does it a bite at a time over a period of weeks and months.

You can digest the library of God's Word. Take a bite at a time from a book at a time, and your understanding will increase as you go. To begin this mastery of the Scriptures, it makes sense to start with a manageably short book of the Bible. Practicing your developing Bible-study techniques on one of the shorter books gives you the satisfaction of completing an initial study of the book in a relatively short time as well as allowing you to see the whole book more quickly.

Toward the end of his life the apostle John wrote the brief book we now call *First John.* In it John shares what he learned through his long friendship with Jesus. Start your Bible reading with this little book.

1. *Read It*—Familiarize yourself with its content.
2. *Listen to It*—Attempt to learn from what you read.
3. *Obey It*—Apply it to your daily context.

(*First John* in special printed form is available. A cassette recorded in a format for faster learning is also available.) Here are four suggestions to help you get as much as possible from *First John.*

Suggestion One: Pretend

Pretend you live in the city of Ephesus near the home of the apostle John. For weeks you've watched him lovingly minister to many. They come to and go from his house at all hours of the day and night. You see he is an ordinary person, similar to you in many ways. But he talks about Jesus as though He is God and his closest friend.

Imagine that one day John explains how you can know God and have eternal life. It is the best news you ever heard! You trust Jesus as your Savior and Lord. You are born from above!

Then you ask John how you can have an intimate friendship with Jesus like he has.

John replies, "Many have asked me this same question. For more than sixty years Jesus has been my Lord and my Best Friend. Before I began to follow Jesus I was in the commercial fishing business with my father and brother. Even after I had been His disciple for a short time I was hot-tempered and had a lot of selfish ambition. I've learned much and I've changed over these more than sixty years. I'm still not all I'm going to be. But when I see Him face to face I will become like Him! I know that day is coming soon.

"Let me take time to pray and think about how to answer you. Then as God enables me, I'll write it down and you will have it to guide you and to share with others even after I go to be with the Lord."

Days later he brings you a small handwritten scroll. Its words share what he has learned through the long years of growing friendship with Jesus. As he hands you the scroll, he says, "Anyone who is in Christ is a new Creation, the old has passed away and the new has come. I remember when Andrew brought his brother to Jesus. The Lord looked at him and said, 'You are Simon but you will be called Peter—a rock!' The Lord gave him a new name. The new name described what the Lord was going to cause him to become. Simon was impulsive and unstable. But Peter was to become stable and solid like bedrock.

"Now that you are 'in Christ' you are a new creation. The Lord God has adopted you into His family. He is the King of Kings and Lord of Lords! And you are His child. You are royalty in the fullest and best sense of the word! You are the King's child. I like the name Kingschild. Sometimes I think of myself as John Kingschild.

"Peter sometimes used his names together. He called himself 'Simon Peter.' This reminded him of what he had been and what he would be.

"You can use your first name as a reminder of what you were before the Lord came into your life. Let me suggest that, just between you and the Lord, you assume a new last name. 'Kingschild' will remind you of what you are now. This will have an effect on how you think and live. Since He has lavished His love on you by bringing you into His family, you don't want to do anything to dishonor His name!

"God has guided me to put on this scroll what I have found helpful in building friendship with Jesus. *Do* what *He* says to you through what I have written. As you obey Him, you will have a life of joy, certainty, victory over circumstances, and will be properly guarded in your faith."

We suggested that you pretend this, but there is more reality to this than make-believe. God did have John write this book for you. So claim these truths as you read *First John*.

Suggestion Two: Pray

Before seeking to digest *First John*, sincerely pray:

Open my eyes, that I may see
Wondrous things from Your law....
Give me understanding,
    and I shall keep Your law;
Indeed, I shall observe it with my
    whole heart (Psalm 119:18,34).

Suggestion Three: Digest

You can read *First John* aloud at one time in about fifteen minutes. It contains concentrated basic truths that are food for your soul. Many find deeper learning tapes* help them digest God's Word. For deeper learning, First John has been divided into ten small "bites." Try to complete at least one bite a day to nourish your soul.

The ten bites are:

1. 1:1–10
2. 2:1–11
3. 2:12–17
4. 2:18–27
5. 2:28–3:10

6. 3:11–20
7. 3:21–4:6
8. 4:7–21
9. 5:1–12
10. 5:13–21

(If you do not use the tape, skip the next four paragraphs and begin reading again with Suggestion Four.)

Each bite has two parts. The first part has four seconds of speaking followed by four of silence. While listening to the speaking, follow the words on the printed page. During the silence, look at the words and think back over what you have just heard. If you are where you can, say the words aloud. Sometimes the reading on the tape will stop before the end of a sentence. This causes your mind to think ahead to finish the thought, especially in the second part of a bite.

Before the second part begins, you should lay aside the printed pages, close your eyes and relax. Then lis-

---

*Deeper learning tapes of *First John* and *First John* in special printed form are available at your local bookstore or through Serve International, P. O. Box 723846, Atlanta, GA 30339.

ten once more to that bite. This time there will be a soft musical background. Concentrate on listening to the music and let your mind absorb the words.

After you listen to a bite a few times, during the silence you will find your mind thinking forward to the next words rather than reflecting back to what you have just heard. Say them aloud and let the tape confirm when you are accurate and correct when you are not accurate.

As you digest *First John* in this manner, seek to apply its truth in your daily life. And remember though you are John Jones or Mary Smith or whatever your name is, you are also John Kingschild or Mary Kingschild!

Suggestion Four: Respond

After you listen to the second part, use whatever time you have left to respond. Open *First John* to the bite you have just digested.

Obeying Jesus from your heart is essential to intimate friendship with Him. Before you can obey from your heart, the truth must pass through three guards that protect your heart (see Chapter 2).

Before you begin reading and listening, get a small notebook. Write your response to the four filter questions listed on pages 26–27 for each bite in the notebook. Once a week, reflect on what God has impressed on your heart and how you are obeying it.

When you write your thinking in the notebook, use your own words. Avoid merely copying John's words. Share your thinking with a Christian friend or your pastor.

To gain the most from *First John*, you should set aside at least fifteen minutes a day, five days a week, for the next two weeks. Pick a time when you can concentrate without interruption in a place that is free from distractions. Think of this as your special appointment with Jesus, a time when He will speak to you through Scripture to deepen your friendship.

In addition to a set time each day, you will want to listen to this tape while you are getting ready for the day, driving to work, preparing meals, and going to sleep at night—any time you are doing something that does not require full use of your mind. But *do this in addition to the set time—never as a substitute for it.*

Jesus spoke the truth when He said, "Without Me you can do nothing" (John 15:5). Paul also spoke the truth when he said, "I can do all things through Christ who strengthens me" (Philippians 4:13). As your friendship with Jesus grows through loving obedience to His Word, His Spirit will do supernatural things in and through you!

Do what Jesus tells you through *First John.* Obey from your heart. By doing what He says, you can have a life of joy, certainty, and victory over circumstances and be properly guarded in your faith.

The Reward of Bible Reading

The benefits of reading God's Word are many. Psalm 119 is a reflection of the practical advantages gained from reading and understanding God's Word. The psalmist says God's Word...

- causes me to be thankful and grateful (v. 7)
- prompts me to live with honor (v. 9)
- deters me from sin and yielding to temptations (v. 11)

- gives me insight into God's promises and plans (v. 18)
- gives me wise counsel about life's decisions (v. 24)
- gives me hope when discouraged (v. 25)
- gives me a greater capacity to obey God (v. 32)
- gives me comfort in times of distress (v. 50)
- enhances my judgment and discernment in life situations (v. 66)
- enables me to stand strong when lies or slanders are told about me by others (v. 69)
- prompts me to refrain from doing things that afterward I would regret and feel ashamed of having done (v. 80)
- gives me insight and wisdom into life beyond my years and experience (v. 99)
- gives me guidance in decisions (v. 105)
- enables me to do what is right (v. 112)
- gives me proper perspective (v. 128)
- gives me God's values as to what He hates and what He loves (v. 163)
- gives me peace even in adversity (v. 165)
- enables me to recall God's promises and to claim them before Him as I lovingly obey Him (v. 173)
- helps me to obey by reminding me of His desires (v. 175)

In other words, the psalmist says God's Word can make you successful.

With proper guidance and obedience to God's Word, Christians are able to experience success in the truest sense. *Success for the Christian is defined as doing God's whole will.* In God's eyes, success is determined by your loving obedience. Success is not determined by the size of your bank account, the number of degrees you have, or your position at work.

Most people who know Tom consider him to be "Mr. Successful." From all outward appearances he is the very image of what our society regards as a true success. From a humble beginning in the mountains of Kentucky, through the hardships of the depression, the struggles of a college education, and the hard, dedicated work at his job, Tom finally reached the zenith. His beautiful, well-dressed wife and children, his large, spacious house in an elite neighborhood, and his fleet of cars signaled success.

But no one could see the loneliness, depression, and unhappiness behind the fake smiles. The absence of a spiritual life was taking its toll on Mr. Successful. He was like the man that Jesus described who had gained the whole world but lost his soul (see Matthew 16:26). Tom's bottom-line profit was zero.

In order to *do* God's will, you must first *know* His will, and knowing God's will comes by reading His Word with understanding. That's why reading the Bible is so important. You read in order to understand His desires. You seek to obey His desires in order to express your gratitude and love to God. Reading God's Word, therefore, is a concrete way of showing your love and desire for Him. Strive to make this a part of your daily routine, and the sense of God's presence will be the reward for your loving obedience.

Next we will look at two more facets of our love for God: meditation and memorization. These are further aids to strengthen and deepen our friendship with the Lord.

Reflections

1. What do I understand this to be saying?

2. What is God telling me to do that I'm not afraid to do?

3. What do I want to understand better?

4. What is God telling me that I find hard to apply to my life?

The Key to Success

5

5   Meditation and Memorization

*A*my was a love-starved young lady whose boy-friend Bill was unaffectionate but always talked about love in glowing terms. One evening Bill told Amy in his usual tirade, "If only I knew how to love you! If I had a thousand arms, I would squeeze you with all of them!"

"I'd be perfectly happy if you would only use the two you have," Amy announced.

How can we love God? We can't put our arms around Him and our words alone don't seem to be a sufficient expression of love. Our best efforts sometime seem so inadequate. In our Christian growth there are some concrete ways in which we can show our love toward Him.

Jesus tells us that the way to grow in intimacy with Him is to lovingly obey His commandments. As we obey these, He reveals more of Himself to us. In the Greatest Commandment, Jesus has given us our guide for expressing love to Him. He said, "Love the Lord your God with all your heart, with all your soul, with all your mind, and with all your strength" (Mark 12:30).

By obeying the Greatest Commandment, we demonstrate our love for God. Our love will manifest itself in various activities. As a husband declares his love for his wife and demonstrates it in tangible ways, so our love for God will take on concrete expression.

Two concrete expressions of love to God are meditation and memorization. The reward for these is a growing sense of intimacy with Jesus.

Four questions will enable you to glean the most from this study. Ask yourself these four questions as you evaluate the thoughts to follow:

1. What do I understand this to be saying?
2. What is God telling me to do that I'm not afraid to try?
3. What do I want to understand better?
4. What is God telling me that I find hard to apply to my life?

Meditation: The Key to Success

Meditation is an important means of increasing our intimacy with Jesus. As a matter of fact, God said it is a precondition for success. To Joshua, the leader of His chosen people, God said, "This Book of the Law shall not depart from your mouth, but you shall meditate in it day and night, that you may observe to do according to all that is written in it. For then you will make your way prosperous, and then you will have good success" (Joshua 1:8).

The key to success is to be discovered in meditation. The Lord was saying, "If you want to have a successful relationship with God and others, then spend time in meditation." Success defined Jesus' way is not money in the bank nor a prestigious title. Success, according to Jesus, is the ability to do all that God commanded. The individual who is able to filter God's Word through his thoughts and into his daily actions is the successful person.

You can be successful. You can accomplish God's whole will when you meditate on God's Word and do what He says.

Meditation

What is meant by the word *meditation?* As you consider it, your mind probably pictures different scenes. Often images from Eastern religions come to mind. Yoga positions and burning incense are Hollywood's images. Differing significantly from these is the Christian meaning of meditation.

In Eastern meditation an individual attempts to empty all thoughts from his mind. All thoughts are to be erased just as words are wiped from a chalkboard. Christian meditation, however, attempts to empty the mind in order to fill it again.

Meditation is not mere reading.

It is not memorization, although you will want to hide these words in your heart from time to time as their personal meaning increases.

Meditation on the Bible means you regard its words as nourishing food. So, with your mind and your heart, "chew" the words of God well. Digest them. Regard them as essential to your well-being. Let God's truths become a part of your life. By faith, use the strength you receive from them to meet the needs you see others wrestling with at home, at work, or in your neighborhood.

The Power of Meditation

Meditation is not meant to be an end in itself. Meditation is a means of gaining God's perspective and power in order to carry out His desires in the world. In meditation, you withdraw from the world for a time so that you can come back into the world and interact with it as Jesus has instructed you. In this way, meditation rejuvenates you to do God's will.

Meditation has the power to redirect your life. As you step away from the business of daily pressures brought on by the tyranny of the urgent, you can gain God's perspective. Meditation helps you see the important tasks amidst the ever-present abundance of urgent demands.

It enables you to deal with human life successfully. Meditation is firmly rooted in reality. In meditation, you present your problems and struggles to God, seeking His perspective and insight. In contemplative prayer, you talk to God about your challenges and listen for His perspective. Jesus wants to know what is on your mind. Then He wants you to gain His perspective on these matters as you talk to Him and listen to Him in meditation.

He will give you the wisdom of His Holy Spirit. In this process your life is given direction and clarity. You are enabled to better know how to specifically obey God in your daily challenges.

In meditation, you engage all of your senses, all of your mental, emotional, and spiritual muscle, in the task of hearing the Lord with your whole being so that you can follow Him with your whole being.

Memorization

Memorization is yet another way to keep in touch with your Best Friend. By memorizing God's Word, you will constantly have His thoughts, His perspective of love toward you, and His wisdom within you for confidence, instruction, and joy.

Usually it takes repeated efforts to memorize Scripture, but once it is embedded in your mind, it becomes almost a permanent fixture never to be forgotten. It is like learning the alphabet. You will use it throughout your entire life. However, at the time you were in the learning process, it may have seemed impossible and unnecessary to agonize through the experience. But now you can see that the lessons you memorized are useful for your enjoyment, communication, and growth.

As you memorize God's Word, the benefits of having God's thoughts readily available increase. For example, when you have to make an important decision, the Holy Spirit can call to your remembrance a memorized passage that has bearing on your decision. As a result you can act more decisively and with a greater sense of confidence.

If you are to be properly guided and protected by God, His Word must be in your mind and heart. The psalmist said: "Your word I have hidden in my heart, that I might not sin against You" (119:11). Since God's first communication with man, He has helped His people store His Word in their hearts so they can know Him more intimately.

Where to Start

There are two types of passages that are especially advantageous for you to memorize: God's *promises* and God's *commandments*.

Here is a promise that you should learn by heart. It is *God's promise of eternal life:* "For God so loved the world that He gave His only begotten Son, that whoever believes in Him should not perish but have everlasting life" (John 3:16).

In an earlier chapter we looked at *two key commandments* that Jesus gave:

> You shall love the Lord your God with all your heart, with all your soul, with all your mind (Matthew 22:37).

> And the second is like it: "You shall love your neighbor as yourself." On these two commandments hang all the Law and the Prophets (Matthew 22:39–40).

Memorize these word for word. Digest them. God will use the promise to give you certainty of eternal life. His promise will also give you the gospel in a nutshell to share with others. The two commandments provide the focus for your life. Knowing the promises of God will give you hope and encouragement.

How easy it is to forget all of the riches of God's promises to us at precisely the time we need them most. Participants in Alcoholics Anonymous, for instance, are very careful to memorize and remind themselves of the promises they are given as they enter into their program of recovery. It is precisely these promises that help them avoid a temptation to pick up the bottle. We too need a memory filled with God's promises and commandments so that we can avoid wandering off the path of righteousness. His commandments as well as His promises give us stability and encouragement as we draw nearer to our Best Friend.

Knowing the commandments of God will give you direction for your life. Thousands of God's people say the words of the first commandment every morning and night as their prayer and declaration of faith. Put the truth of the previous three verses together. Say them every morning and night as your prayer and declaration of faith. Do this until these truths are planted deep in your heart and soul. Do this until these truths automatically shape your behavior.

Here is one way you can form these words into your personal prayer and statement of faith.

> God, You loved me so much You sent Jesus, Your one and only Son. I believe what Jesus taught is true. Because I believe Him I will never be separated from You. Instead, I will live with You forever.

> Lord, You are my God! With Your help, I will love You with all my desires and with all my soul and with all my thoughts and with all my strength. With Your help, I will love my neighbor as much as I love myself.

If you make these a part of your thinking, these truths will automatically begin to shape your behavior. You will find that your knowledge of your Best Friend will grow. With this knowledge you will notice a slow and steady change in your life. The quality and wisdom of your decisions will improve as you increase in a maturing relationship with Jesus. The knowledge gained through this process of memorization will build you gradually. But knowledge can also produce arrogance. In your desire to learn more, be careful to balance your knowledge with self-sacrificing service and love (see 1 Corinthians 8:1).

As your knowledge of God increases through meditation and memorization, so will your relationship and intimacy with Jesus. You can be successful in the eyes of God if you think of His Word and hide His Word in your life. In addition to these, memorizing God's Word will affect your life in yet another way.

Memorization enables you to pray more effectively. You can apply the promises of God to your requests and intercessions. Knowing what God's Word says will help you to pray with power. For if you ask anything in agreement with His will, He promises to give it (see John 14:13).

Many people find it hard to memorize words. If this is true for you, let me suggest a method that will make it not only easy but also fun! You will find it described in the Appendix.

In addition to meditation and memorization, God has told us how we can get to know Him better through yet another means. We'll consider how prayer enables us to grow more intimate with God in Chapter 6.

Reflections

1. What do I understand this to be saying?

   That I need to arm myself with the word of God & meditate on it if I want to win my battles

2. What is God telling me to do that I'm not afraid to do? *To read his truths*

3. What do I want to understand better?

   The depth of God's love for me, and maybe the reason for it

4. What is God telling me that I find hard to apply to my life? *to let go of my fears & trust in Him*

To Whom
It May Concern?!

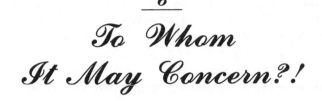

6 **Prayer**

"*J*ean, this is Joyce," she said quickly over the
phone. "I've just finished baking your wonder-
ful homemade rolls, and they are a complete flop."

"What went wrong?" Jean asked.

"I wish I knew. I followed the recipe I copied at your
house the other night, but they sure didn't turn out like
yours."

"Maybe we better go over that recipe again," suggested Jean. Sure enough, in her haste, Joyce failed to
include one very important ingredient, which caused
the entire experience to fail.

If you've ever attempted to make an omelette, you
know that the one ingredient you cannot leave out and
still succeed is the eggs. An omelette is not an omelette
without eggs. What is the most essential ingredient in a

meaningful relationship which when omitted leaves no relationship? That one ingredient is communication. If communication ceases, then two people begin to drift apart, and their relationship diminishes over time. A meaningful relationship cannot exist without communication. God communicates with us through His Holy Spirit, especially when we read the Bible, meditate on His words, and memorize them for later recall. We communicate with God through prayer.

God wants to speak to you. As your Best Friend, He desires to reveal more of Himself to you. In like fashion He wants you to reveal more of yourself to Him. Through prayer, you can reveal your innermost thoughts and requests to Him and you can talk intimately with Him.

Listen to these thoughts on prayer through the filter of four important questions:

1. What do I understand this to be saying?
2. What is God telling me to do that I'm not afraid to try?
3. What do I want to understand better?
4. What is God telling me that I find hard to apply to my life?

These questions, when answered truthfully and carefully, will help you personalize these thoughts for yourself.

How to Pray

Prayer is a way to thank Jesus for specific things He has done for you and others you love. It is also a way to communicate to Him your needs for help. All people have an instinct to pray. It's part of God's image in us. The non-Christian native in a remote jungle prays to several gods. The soldier in a foxhole calls out to God to save him in a time of emergency. But apart from living trust in Jesus, prayer is much like putting a note in a bottle and throwing it into the sea. The sender hopes it will reach its destination, but he is not sure it will. Prayer apart from living trust in Jesus is a form of wishful thinking addressed "to whom it may concern."

In contrast, prayer combined with living trust and loving obedience is like an arrow fired at a specific target with accuracy and power. Our prayer is never addressed "to whom it may concern"; it is directed to "our Father in heaven." Because He is our Father, we have all the more reason to trust Him; we ask Him as His children.

Prayer is addressed to God. God is alive and living. Consequently, you can enter into living, personal contact with Him. You can talk with Him just as people did when He was on earth. God is a person. Therefore, pray in a personal, specific fashion. Be aware that you are speaking to a personal, caring God. He is not an impersonal answering machine.

When praying to your Best Friend, call Him by name. Jesus said, "Until now you have asked nothing in My name. Ask, and you will receive, that your joy may be full" (John 16:24).

As you pray to your Best Friend, pray expectantly, trusting Him to respond as you ask. Doubt displeases Him (see James 1:6). Ask Him with confidence and He will answer. If you have noticed the implicit faith and trust of young children, you will begin to understand why that sort of childlike trust is so pleasing to our Father in heaven, as the following vignette illustrates.

A family planned a picnic one afternoon. As the time approached for them to leave, they noticed rain clouds gathering. The youngest daughter suggested that they pray and ask God to hold back the rain for their picnic. They all prayed, asking God to provide nice weather for their outing. They packed the lunch and loaded the car. On the way out the door, the father grabbed an umbrella. The little girl, noticing this, looked up at her father and said, "Dad, we don't need that. Don't you believe God will hold back the rain like we asked?"

The little girl's confidence is an example of the kind of faith that pleases God. Pray confidently, anticipating His response. After all, He is your Best Friend!

Jesus spent much time talking to His Father. His disciples realized that compared to Him they did not know how to pray. So they asked Him to teach them, and He did. He showed them that prayer did not have to take place in a church building. It can take place anywhere (see Genesis 24:26,63). Jesus Himself prayed on boats, in homes, on mountains, and on the cross.

Jesus also gave His friends a model of what to pray for. Jesus said,

> In this manner, therefore, pray:
>
> Our Father in heaven,
> Hallowed be Your name.
> Your kingdom come.
> Your will be done
> On earth as it is in heaven.
> Give us this day our daily bread.
> And forgive us our debts,
> As we forgive our debtors.
> And do not lead us into temptation,
> But deliver us from the evil one.

For Yours is the kingdom and the
power and the glory forever.
Amen (Matthew 6:9–13).

Jesus' model illustrates that our prayers can cover all our concerns and those of our friends. Prayer can be about anything, from the smallest matter to the greatest, from the affairs of today to those of eternity. Nothing is too small and nothing is too large to ask for your Best Friend's help. The Old Testament book of Psalms, primarily a collection of prayers, illustrates this very fact.

The Holy Spirit Will Help You Pray

Today, by His Spirit, Jesus continues to help us. Scripture explains, "The Spirit also helps in our weaknesses. For we do not know what we should pray for as we ought, but the Spirit Himself makes intercession for us with groanings which cannot be uttered" (Romans 8:26). The Holy Spirit takes our imperfect prayers and offers them in perfect fashion before our heavenly Father. How does He do this?

Bob Biehl, in his helpful book *Praying, How to Start and Keep Going,* mentions the story of the world-famous pianist Ignacy Paderewski. It seems he was scheduled to give a performance at a London concert hall one evening. In the middle of the bare platform stood one large grand piano with a spotlight trained on it, ready for the artist's gifted touch. A half-hour before he was to appear, the hall was already packed. Celebrities and dignitaries in elegant evening clothes were everywhere.

One admiring mother had paid the full adult price for her seven-year-old son to attend. She knew he would practice with greater interest if he could only hear the accomplished pianist. In the excitement of conversation with friends, however, the mother had not noticed that her son had slipped out of his seat.

Suddenly the sound of a piano drifted out over the immediately hushed crowd. The mother looked on stage and there sat her son on the piano bench prepared for Paderewski. He was playing "Chopsticks"!

Someone from the crowd cried out, "Chopsticks! Get that kid down!"

The embarrassed mother started down the crowded aisle, pleading apologetically, "Please let me through. That's my son!"

As she made her way to the front, Paderewski quietly slipped out and sat by the boy as he played. Instead of scolding, he encouraged him. "Keep going, boy," he said. "Don't stop now. I'll help you. Keep going." He joined in the music, filling in around the boy's simple tune. His runs and key work produced a masterpiece that thrilled the audience.

Often when we pray, we may feel as if we are playing "Chopsticks." The Holy Spirit, however, takes our feeble efforts and produces a masterpiece before God. He encourages us, "Keep going! Don't stop now!"

The more your prayer life develops, the more you will know of God. You learn about God through prayer. Prayer is not a monologue; it is a dialogue. During your prayers, there will often be moments of silence so that you can listen to Jesus' words and commands. Prayer is a genuine conversation with Jesus that you learn to have with increasing ease. Yet the more you learn, the more you know you have yet to learn. A child playing at the seashore knows a little about the ocean. If she studies the ocean all her life, she may become an expert compared to other people. But the more she studies the ocean, the more she knows she has yet to learn about the ocean. So it is with prayer. A person who is really growing in his prayer life is always humbled by what he has yet to learn.

Our heavenly Father has many good things to give us and many good experiences to teach us through prayer.

How Loving Obedience Affects Your Prayers

There are many things that could be said about prayer. But for developing friendship through loving obedience, one word needs to be emphasized here.

The apostle John said: "Beloved, if our heart does not condemn us, we have confidence toward God. And whatever we ask we receive from Him, *because we keep His commandments and do those things that are pleasing in His sight*" (1 John 3:21–22, italics added). When we "keep His commandments and do those things that are pleasing in His sight," He answers prayer. The diagram "Conditions to Effective Prayer" offers guidance on how to pray.

The first prerequisite to answered prayer is a lifestyle marked by loving obedience to God's commands.

As we obey Jesus and see Him answer our prayers, we will sense His presence in a deeper way. Jesus Himself said, "And He who sent Me is with Me. The Father has not left Me alone, for I always do those things that please Him" (John 8:29).

Jesus experienced the presence and power of His Father here on earth as He lovingly obeyed Him. We too

CONDITIONS TO EFFECTIVE PRAYER

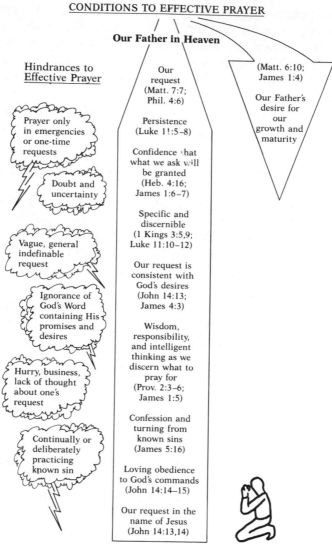

Our Father in Heaven

Hindrances to
Effective Prayer

Prayer only
in emergencies
or one-time
requests

Doubt and
uncertainty

Vague, general
indefinable
request

Ignorance of
God's Word
containing His
promises and
desires

Hurry, business,
lack of thought
about one's
request

Continually or
deliberately
practicing
known sin

Our
request
(Matt. 7:7;
Phil. 4:6)

Persistence
(Luke 11:5-8)

Confidence that
what we ask will
be granted
(Heb. 4:16;
James 1:6-7)

Specific and
discernible
(1 Kings 3:5,9;
Luke 11:10-12)

Our request is
consistent with
God's desires
(John 14:13;
James 4:3)

Wisdom,
responsibility,
and intelligent
thinking as we
discern what to
pray for
(Prov. 2:3-6;
James 1:5)

Confession and
turning from
known sins
(James 5:16)

Loving obedience
to God's commands
(John 14:14–15)

Our request in the
name of Jesus
(John 14:13,14)

(Matt. 6:10;
James 1:4)

Our Father's
desire for
our
growth and
maturity

will experience God's presence and power in our lives as we obey Him. The by-product will be a greater sense of confidence and boldness in our daily living. As we obey His commands and gain a greater awareness of His presence, we will experience a degree of confidence unknown before in our prayers.

As we grow in confidence that our prayers are heard, the result will be a greater degree of joy in our lives (see John 16:24). Our sense of expectation will also rise as we make requests that are quite specific and expectant of God's help.

As we obey Him, we will increasingly surround all our activities and choices with prayer. Prayer is the activity that rounds out the relationship God desires of us. When we pray, we commune with God and share out of our deepest being what we have learned of God through meditating on His Word and what desires are growing within us from that meditation. Along with that, we have the inestimable privilege of sensing His living presence within us as we wait in silence for His affirming word, His consoling touch, His challenge, or whatever we most need from Him as we pray. It is no wonder that we will wish to live less and less of our lives "on our own" the more we enter into prayer.

Jesus knows and cares about every minute detail of our lives. We can ask Him about our participating in various activities and call upon His direction for decisions, big or small, that we are asked to make.

As we do this, our anxieties will diminish (see Philippians 4:6), and our awareness of our Best Friend's presence will increase. Prayer is an essential ingredient that enables our relationship with Jesus to grow.

While our words help us to communicate our love to

God, our actions send significant messages to God too. God understands that our priorities in life reveal our genuine affections. Therefore, in the next chapter, we will discuss how the establishment of proper priorities is a vital means of expressing our love to God.

Reflections

1. What do I understand this to be saying? I need to stay in touch with God if I want to feel close to him I need to memorize his word so I can meditate on it + recall it + believe it.

2. What is God telling me to do that I'm not afraid to do? To come closer to him

3. What do I want to understand better? What love really is.

4. What is God telling me that I find hard to apply to my life? Allowing myself to be loved according to other peoples definitions instead of my own.

Keeping Your Loves in Line

7

7 Proper Priorities

*D*on became an enthusiastic new Christian four months ago. In his zeal, he had gotten carried away. It seemed as though he was involved in every church activity he could find. On weekends, he helped take care of the church grounds. He volunteered to drive the church bus and was now involved in Bible studies two nights a week.

His wife and children had been praying for his salvation for several years. Before he trusted Christ, he always had time for family outings, and he would make a special point to spend time with Helen, his wife. Now, he and his family were frustrated. He couldn't find enough time and energy to do everything he wanted to do.

Don approached his pastor one Sunday and explained his situation. "I feel so confused right now. I am torn in so many directions. How can I prioritize my life so that the most important things are not crowded out?" he asked.

The implications of the Greatest Commandment have far-reaching effects on our lives. The command to love the Lord our God with all of our heart, our soul, our mind, and our strength affects each area of our lives.

Perhaps you have noticed some areas of your life that have undergone changes since you have known Jesus. In other areas you are just beginning to feel challenged. You are involved in a lifetime process whereby Jesus is enabling you to become more like Him. Part of what it means to be His friend is that you take on His values. An important part of Jesus' life was the establishment of proper priorities. Without priorities He would not have made it to the cross. Many distractions were there to tempt Him away from His goal. The most important priority in His life was maintaining the relationship He had with His Father in heaven.

Through that relationship, He was directed in the use of His time. When He died at the age of thirty-three, He could say, "It is finished" (John 19:30). He finished everything He came to do. Because His relationship with the Father was His number one priority, He knew when to worship and when to work. He knew when to take time with His close friends and when to minister to the masses. He knew when to be gentle and when to be stern.

The relationship with His Father was the center, the hub, of His life. All other areas of importance emanated from that hub, like spokes on a wheel. He let the

Father move Him through life, from birth to death. And He always did the right thing at the right time.

Know Your Competition

As you become a friend of Jesus, your top priority should be to maintain your relationship with Him. To Moses, God expressed His desire in the negative: "You shall have no other gods before Me" (Exodus 20:3). He alone is to have the first place in your life! You tell Jesus He has top priority in your life by giving His desires precedence in time, order, and importance over your competing self-pleasing interests. God is not impressed when you offer Him your leftovers. Only offer Him your best.

Eric Liddell, the Olympic runner and inspiration for the movie *Chariots of Fire*, was faced with a decision of priority when he was told he was to run the finals of his Olympic race on Sunday. To Eric, Sunday was the Lord's Day. It was a day for worship and rest. Even though he felt that God had placed him in a unique position of witness with his running speed, Eric refused to compromise his beliefs. He declined to run the race on Sunday.

Eric had trained for years to reach the Olympics and was physically ready for the competition. When a decision had to be made, he did not hesitate to give God the first priority in his life. History records that on another day he ran a different race for which he had not trained, yet he won the gold medal anyway.

For Eric Liddell, prestige and public recognition competed with God for first place in his life. What are some of the things competing for first place in your life? What are other loves that tend to divide your attention and loyalty from God? As a human being, you need food, drink, clothing, and shelter, but each of these can become a pursuit that crowds Jesus out of the place of utmost importance in your life.

Food can become a first love when you cannot say no to it. Bob has made food his top priority, though it is difficult for him to admit. He is constantly seeking new taste treats. He is dangerously overweight, but if he sees an enticing dessert in a display window, he simply has to try it.

Clothes can be a first love if you must always have the "right look" or wear the latest style. Faye is a young woman who is constantly looking for the latest clothing styles in magazines, store displays, and fashion shows. When she sees a particular dress, skirt, or blouse, she knows it is just right for her. Of course she must have matching shoes, purse, and jewelry, and she is willing to skimp on her food, pay her rent late, or postpone her other bill payments in order to acquire the latest fashion. Her closets are overflowing with new outfits. Yet her insatiable desires lead her on to buy more.

Shelter can become a god if all of your time and energy is taken to maintain your home. Doug and Joan are continually trying to upgrade their home and neighborhood to impress others. In so doing they are placing greater priority on pursuing prestige than on pursuing God. Jesus says, "For the pagans run after all these things, and your heavenly Father knows that you need them. But seek first his kingdom and his righteousness, and all these things will be given to you as well" (Matthew 4:10 NIV).

Satan tempted Jesus with wealth and power. But

Jesus said to him, "Away with you, Satan! For it is written, 'You shall worship the LORD your God, and Him only you shall serve' " (Matthew 4:10).

The desire to accumulate wealth or to gain power and prestige can easily and subtly become your priority. Some historians believe President Nixon's downfall came as a result of his desire for power and prestige. They believe it was his desire to secure these that led to Watergate. He believed that the inside information he gained would assure his election victory. If this is true, the desire for power and prestige apparently took first place in his life and eventually led to his downfall.

If we cannot say no to something, it controls us and becomes our top priority.

The Problem with Divided Loyalties: Indecisiveness

Jesus pointedly states, "You cannot serve two masters: God and money. For you will hate one and love the other, or else the other way around" (Matthew 6:24 TLB). Jesus does not share first place with any other person or desire.

God commands us to love Him with our *whole* heart. When we allow other loves to compete with His prominence, then we suffer from a divided heart.

A fierce little terrier had caught an unsuspecting sparrow in his backyard. Several of the little bird's friends flew closer and closer to the terrier, trying to divert his attention from the captive sparrow. When they surrounded him, chirping loudly with gesturing motions, the little dog lunged toward the closest sparrow, snapping to catch another bird. In his attempt he released the captive bird, and they all flew away in safety. No one had told the little terrier that "a bird in the hand is worth two in the bush."

The Bible says that a double-minded man is unstable in all his ways (see James 1:8). In Matthew we have the story of Jesus' encounter with a man who had just such a disease. All the telltale signs were evident.

> Now behold, one came to Him, "Good Teacher, what good thing shall I do that I may have eternal life?" So He said to him, "Why do you call Me good? No one is good but One, that is, God. But if you want to enter into life, keep the commandments." He said to Him, "Which ones?" Jesus said, " 'You shall not murder,' 'You shall not steal,' 'You shall not bear false witness,' 'Honor your father and your mother,' and, 'You shall love your neighbor as yourself.' " The young man said to Him, "All these things I have kept from my youth. What do I still lack?" Jesus said to him, "If you want to be perfect, go, sell what you have and give to the poor, and you will have treasure in heaven; and come, follow Me." But when the young man heard that saying, he went away sorrowful, for he had great possessions. Then Jesus said to His disciples, "Assuredly, I say to you that it is hard for a rich man to enter the kingdom of heaven" (Matthew 19:16–23).

The rich young ruler had a divided heart. He desired eternal life, but in this test it was evident he loved his wealth more. Jesus looked at the competing love in his life and diagnosed it as wealth. To test which he was more devoted to, Jesus asked him to surrender his wealth. This the rich man would not do and went away "sorrowful."

Is there anything you would have difficulty surrendering if Jesus asked you to? If there is, then you have identified the love that competes for first place in your life. In and of themselves there is probably nothing wrong with these items. But when they take the place Jesus demands, they become divisive.

A Proper View of Money

Twin brothers, Tom and Terry, worked side by side in developing a new computer program that would simplify an otherwise complicated bookkeeping system. Through their intense marketing, sales skyrocketed, and profits to the brothers were beyond their wildest imaginations.

With his portion, Tom said, "This is my money, and I intend to buy all of the things I've always wanted."

On the other hand, Terry recognized that everything he had gained had come from God. The money he had was not his money but God's. As God's steward he dedicated it to provide for his family and used what he had to advance Christ's kingdom by helping others.

Which of the two brothers had the proper perspective about wealth?

There is nothing wrong with wealth in itself. God Himself gives the ability to produce wealth (see Deuteronomy 8:1–8). However, if that power is used for selfish ends, the desire for gain takes God's place, and the Greatest Commandment is violated. The divided heart leaves little room for Jesus.

When we love God, we give Him credit for any achievement or financial gain coming from our work because we understand how dependent we are upon His mercy and favor toward us. We also realize that the very gifts and talents which enable us to achieve what we achieve are His gifts to us, not talents we generate on our own. Therefore, we belong totally to God. Our money is God's money, entrusted to us as His stewards. If we use money as though it is ours alone, we abuse our role as stewards. The outcome of such abuse is a gradual relinquishing of your power over money until money eventually gains power over you.

Love of money often chokes out our love for God (see Luke 8:14). That is why we cannot serve both God and money. Many succumb to the gradual process where the love of money becomes their first desire. For every one thousand God can entrust with poverty, He can trust only one with wealth.

Money is not evil. But the *love of money*, whether a small or large amount, "is a root of all kinds of evil" (1 Timothy 6:10). Jesus urges us,

> Do not lay up for yourselves treasures on earth, where moth and rust destroy and where thieves break in and steal; but lay up for yourselves treasures in heaven, where neither moth nor rust destroys and where thieves do not break in and steal. For where your treasure is, there your heart will be also" (Matthew 6:19–21).

Have you ever seen a hearse towing a U-haul? We cannot accumulate worldly wealthy and take it with us when we die. Therefore, Jesus urges us to spend our time and energy on things that will matter long after we have gone. Energy focused on obeying God's commandments rather than accumulating material goods will yield eternal benefits. Jesus also points out that our desires, energies, and time seem to be allotted to those things we value most. Our behavior will always indicate our true priorities.

Accepting the Challenge

The Christian classic *In His Steps* by Charles L. Sheldon has a subtitle, "What Would Jesus Do?" An entire church was challenged to ask that question before making any decision, whether great or small. The result was a spiritual revival and a period of spiritual growth among participating Christians that turned the whole town toward Christ.

Suppose you asked, "What would Jesus do?" before every decision you made. If you were honest in applying God's principles, you would find that competing priorities would diminish. Christ would have the highest priority.

As your Friend, Jesus can help you put money in a proper perspective. Before the coming of Christ, God required His people to bring a *tithe*. A tithe was 10 percent of all they made, and they put it into a storehouse to support His ministry among them (see Malachi 3:6–10). God's people were asked to return a portion of their wealth. They gave a portion back to God as an acknowledgment of His initial provision for them. They gave, seeing their sacrifice as an opportunity to trust Him to provide for their needs.

In the New Testament, Christians are urged to go beyond the tithe. Generosity is one mark of Jesus' friends. We are to give regularly in proportion to His blessing (see 1 Corinthians 16:2). We are not to give reluctantly or under compulsion, "for God loves a cheerful giver" (2 Corinthians 9:7).

Financial giving expresses our reliance on God for both this world and the next. When we give sacrificially, we rely on God to provide and not on our own resources. He promises to supply our needs if we will obey Him in the financial area of our lives. Are you already giving at least a tithe? If not, try it for a three-month period. Most people who try this find the benefits to their spiritual life so great that they continue the practice for the rest of their lives.

Because you are a friend of Jesus, your establishing proper priorities is a means of expressing your love and gratitude to Him. He longs to know that He is your first and greatest desire. With this incentive, spend some time this week reflecting on your loves and desires. Where does Jesus rate in your life's desires? Begin your assessment with your finances and then consider your time expenditures. God will honestly reward those who put Him first with a greater sense of His presence than ever before.

What else increases your sense of God's presence in your life? Worship is another facet of loving obedience we'll consider in Chapter 8.

Reflections

1. What do I understand this to be saying?

   To think about my priorities & where god fits in.

2. What is God telling me to do that I'm not afraid to do?

3. What do I want to understand better?

4. What is God telling me that I find hard to apply to my life?

8

Beyond Ritual and Formality

8   Worship

*F*irst it began with a casual glance, then a brief introduction and reciprocal smiles. Before long, Brad noticed a special attraction to the petite, blue-eyed Donna, and eventually he asked her for a date. After the first few weeks of dating her, his thoughts continued to revolve around her, and he saw her as often as he could.

"It must be love," he mused, because he couldn't seem to get her out of his mind. When he first awakened in the morning, throughout the day and evening, he thought about Donna. During the months that followed, his love continued to grow, and everything he did was designed to please her.

On a scale of one to seven, seven being seldom and one being every minute, how often would you say you sensed the presence of Jesus in your life this past week? How often did He come to mind? How often did you desire to be with Him? Do you want to get to know your Best Friend to the same degree that King David wanted to know Him and be with Him? David said,

> O God, You are my God;
> Early will I seek You;
> My soul thirsts for You;
> My flesh longs for You
> In a dry and thirsty land
> Where there is no water (Psalm 63:1)

God desires to be close and intimate, to be your Best Friend. How strong is your desire to know Him?

Friendships are dynamic; they are either growing or weakening. Your friendship with Jesus is the same way. The means by which you grow in your relationship with Jesus is through loving obedience. As you obey Him by reading His thoughts in the Bible; as you obey Him by meditating on His words and memorizing them; as you obey Him by talking with Him in prayer; as you obey Him by making Him the greatest desire in your life, He reveals more of Himself to you, and you will know Him more intimately.

Let's consider another expression of love to God, our worship of Him. As we consider worship, let's evaluate it in the light of four questions:

1. What do I understand this to be saying?
2. What is God telling me to do that I'm not afraid to try?
3. What do I want to understand better?
4. What is God telling me that I find hard to apply to my life?

What is Worship?

The Sunday bulletin announced "Worship 11 A.M." The Peterson family took their seats in the beautiful sanctuary and prepared themselves for a worshipful service. They sang two songs that were followed by announcements, the offering, and a soloist; the sermon's theme was the current threat of nuclear war and a call for peace. The name of Jesus, the heavenly Father, and the Holy Spirit were seldom mentioned. The benediction was pronounced, and the church quickly emptied as people hurried to lunch. The Petersons drove away in disappointment. Though it was called a worship service, it had been far from worshipful. Worship had evaporated only to leave rituals and formalities. The Petersons left wondering what worship really was. They knew what it was not after this experience.

As they drove home after church, little Robbie asked, "Dad, was that worship? What do they mean by worship?" Many churches today have forgotten the true meaning of worship and have instead adopted the easier planned rituals of a Sunday morning meeting of their members.

What is worship? The word *worship* originally came from the word *worthship*. When we worship our Best Friend, we are attributing "worth" to Him. Worship is honor and adoration we give to God. It may be expressed in many ways, as individuals and as a group. When we have meaningful individual worship, it will deepen our time of group worship in the local church. When each of us has a regular, meaningful time with God on a daily basis, we will find great delight in coming together with His people to worship Him.

The friends of Jesus in the early church met in the temple, in synagogues, and especially in their homes to worship the Lord. He was their Father. They were His family. By gathering to worship, they honored Him. They listened to Him in the preaching and teaching of His Word. They sang songs ascribing honor and thankfulness to Him for what they had seen Him do in their lives that week. They prayed together. In their times of group worship they found direction for their individual and group decisions.

Worship can best be summed up in one word: *giving.* At the heart of our worship should be our giving to God. Unfortunately, so much of our focus during our worship opportunities is on "what are we *getting?*" Not long ago a creative editorial appeared in a Boston paper. Its innovative idea was to critique the worship services of local churches like movies are reviewed. Each church would be rated from one to four stars, based on the performance of the choir, the eloquence and fervor of the preacher, the friendliness of the congregation, and the overall beauty of the church. The rating of the service would be according to how "entertained" the worshiper had been. An entertainment focus reflects an attitude of taking from God rather than giving to God.

Many people unconsciously compare worship services to theatrical performances. They view the preacher as the performer, God the coach in the wings, and the audience the critic. But if this comparison is to be properly made, the roles must change. The preacher becomes the coach, the congregation the performer, and God the critic, the evaluator of the praise. In fact, God does more than merely evaluate. Psalm 22:3 says that He actually is enthroned in the praises of His people! We praise Him and He is powerfully present in our midst. Many people who flounder in their individual worship can become strengthened by this corporate worship, this habitation of God!

The proper focus of our worship is God. The emphasis is on what we can give to Him.

Hindrances to Avoid

We must be on guard against several hindrances to good worship experiences. The temptation to focus on yourself is one such hindrance. Self-preoccupation will obscure God's presence. During the sermon, the Smith family sat quietly, looking blankly at the pastor like a group of statues. Each one was thinking separate thoughts about Sunday afternoon activities. Johnnie mused about the baseball game he would play in at 2 P.M. Sandy was planning the activities for the afternoon with her girlfriends. Mr. Smith wondered if the paperboy threw the newspaper in the wet gutter again, and Mrs. Smith was trying to remember if she set the automatic oven at the right time and temperature.

During worship do you ever let your mind drift away from God to your own interests? Do you allow your preoccupation to obscure God's presence?

Another hindrance to avoid is focusing on others immediately around us. We must not let others distract our attention. We worship God with our whole selves—spirit, soul, and body. If we are focusing on others at worship, for that moment of time we have stopped worshiping God. Obviously, we cannot avoid that once in a while, but if we aren't on guard, we might find ourselves observing worship rather than actually entering into the activity of worship.

A third distraction in our group worship is our tendency to quickly focus on the imperfections around us. A choir member may be off-key, the piano may be out of tune, the pastor may not be as eloquent as you prefer. Local churches have only imperfect people like you and me in them. But when we come together and worship God in spirit and truth, we become more of what God desires us to be, as individuals and as a group. As we focus on giving our praise, thanksgiving, worship, and adoration to God, we spend less time focusing on the imperfect things.

Helps to Worship

Whatever local church you are in, it is important to keep in mind the big picture of what the one true Church is becoming. The apostle John, looking into the future, described it as "a great multitude which no one could number, of all nations, tribes, peoples, and tongues, standing before the throne and before the Lamb, clothed with white robes.... Therefore they are before the throne of God, and serve Him day and night in His temple" (Revelation 7:9,15). Jesus promised: "I will build My Church, and the gates of Hades shall not prevail against it" (Matthew 16:18).

The Church is not the building you meet in. It is a collection of all the people in the world, past, present, and future, who have called Jesus their Savior, Lord, and Best Friend. Worship cannot be isolated or regulated to just one place, time, or segment of your life. You cannot verbally praise God in church and display selfishness and jealously outside of church. That kind of effort at worship is a perversion (see Romans 6:13,19). Real acts of worship are the overflow of a worshiping life.

Loving God with *all* extends beyond set times of individual and group worship. Worship is not what you do for an hour in church. Nor is it the few minutes you may give to personal devotions during the week. True worship touches every area and activity of your life (Romans 12:1). Scripture urges, "Whatever you do in word or deed, do all in the name of the Lord Jesus, giving thanks to God the Father through Him" (Colossians 3:17). God wants to be involved in every part of your life—personal, family, business, and social. Your lifestyle is an opportunity to worship God. Choose actions that would reflect what Jesus would choose to do in these areas. When you live by convictions that reflect God's beliefs rather than self-interests, you are worshiping Him.

For Jim Hershel, worshiping God in his business meant a tough decision. Jim purchased a successful hotel with a restaurant and bar. Jim decided the bar was something in his business that did not honor God. He called his manager in one day and shared his convictions. He told the manager that his desire to please God had led him to the decision to close the bar. Surprised, the manager told him that the profit from the bar was what made the operation the success it was. His response was that if Jim closed it, he would be out of business within two months. Jim thanked him for his input, but he stuck with his convictions. The manager immediately resigned. Jim turned the bar into a coffee shop, and the new shop succeeded in producing more income than the bar had. God honored Jim who had honored Him. Not all stories of worshiping God have such endings. Some recount only the cost involved in honoring God.

For Jack, who owned a chain of drug stores, his decision to love God resulted in financial loss. His stores carried several magazines which were pornographic. When he became a Christian he decided these were not pleasing to God. He took a moral stand and had them removed from the shelves. There were financial losses as a result, but Jack had demonstrated his love for God. Loving God does not mean that God will change our circumstances or bring only good things our way, but that God will increase our ability to live above our circumstances. Remember, we worship God through our lifestyles, not just in our church services.

Worship and the Second Greatest Commandment

The second greatest commandment implies a lifestyle of worship. Jesus said the second commandment is like the first—meaning it is of equal value. The second commandment is to "love your neighbor as yourself."

When Jesus said, "Love your neighbor," a listener asked, "And who is my neighbor?" In reply Jesus told the story of the good Samaritan (see Luke 10:27–35). A man went from Jerusalem to Jericho. Robbers stripped him, beat him, and left him half-dead. Religious leaders passed by but refused to get involved. Then a Samaritan (a racially mixed person despised by the Jews) saw him. He felt compassion, bandaged the man's wounds, transported him to safety, and assumed financial responsibility for the care the injured man needed until he was well.

Actually in Jesus' reply He never defined who one's "neighbor" is. Instead He raised a more important question, which of these three do you think was neighbor to him who fell among the thieves?" Of course the answer was, "He who showed mercy on him" (Luke 10:37). Therefore, Jesus seems to indicate *my neighbor is anyone in need.* Sometimes this is a fellow member of God's family. Other times it is a nonbeliever. It may even be an enemy. Kindness shown to others in need is an act of worship to God.

Love for your neighbor will especially show itself among God's family. John the apostle asked Christians, "He who does not love his brother whom he has seen, how can he love God whom he has not seen?" (1 John 4:20).

Worshiping Jesus is expressed through your behavior at home, in the office, and over the backyard fence with your neighbor. In addition to a time of group worship in church, your lifestyle is also an important form of worship you give to God to show your love to Him.

Loving your neighbor as an act of worship to your Friend Jesus is expressed through four dimensions— *fellowship, forgiveness, service,* and *witness.*

In order to better describe these four dimensions, the next three chapters will be devoted to these topics.

Reflections

1. What do I understand this to be saying?

   We are suppose to go to church w/an attitude of giving, not of what we will get out of it. The more time we spend in individual worship the more meaningful group worship will become.

2. What is God telling me to do that I'm not afraid to do? *To start going to church with a different attitude.*

3. What do I want to understand better?

4. What is God telling me that I find hard to apply to my life?

   To keep my focus on Him at all times.

PART III | *Following Through on Your Friendship with God*

A Family of Friends

9   Fellowship

*H*ow can we develop our relationship with Jesus so that we can sense His presence in a close, intimate, and personal way? How can we increase our awareness of His presence in our lives over last week? How can it become a natural part of our thinking to consider Jesus as our Best Friend? Is a moment-by-moment awareness of His presence available to us? Jesus tells us "Yes!" As we lovingly obey Him, He promises to reveal Himself to us (see John 14:21). He promises our friendship with Him will grow.

How can we experience this? Loving obedience is the key. Let's focus on another facet of loving obedience. How can we obey God in the areas of fellowship and forgiveness?

As we consider these new facets, let's evaluate them with four questions in mind:

1. What do I understand this to be saying?
2. What is God telling me to do that I'm not afraid to try?

3. What do I want to understand better?
4. What is God telling me that I find hard to apply to my life?

The Meaning of Fellowship

Fellowship has been described as "fellows in a ship." On board a ship passengers have several things in common. They all have the same destination. If the boat sinks, they all go down. If it reaches its destination, they all get there. They all have the same captain whom they trust. Cooperation on the part of all is necessary for the smooth operation of the boat. In our fellowship with other Christians, we also have several things in common. Our destination is the same, our captain is the same, but we have a tie that binds us together much greater than fellows in a ship.

As we become friends with Jesus, His friends become our friends. We get to know His friends through local church families. We may be on a bus or a plane or in a store and discover someone we can easily befriend all because we both have Jesus as our Best Friend. The friends of Jesus hold something very valuable in common—we have experienced His love. Because we have mutually experienced His love, we can love one another. Our friendships with one another find their source in the common love of Jesus toward us. The Bible tells us, "If God so loved us, we also ought to love one another" (1 John 4:11), and "We love because He first loved us" (1 John 4:19 NASB).

Another benefit of friendship with Jesus is that we are freed from isolation and individualism. As we invite Jesus to be our Best Friend, He adopts us into His family. One means of showing love and gratitude to

Jesus is by entering into mutual fellowship with others Jesus has adopted into His family.

God desires constructive interaction between His friends who have different personalities and cultural backgrounds. Jesus looks forward to the day when all of His friends who comprise the true Church will be with Him in heaven. At that time there will be people from every nation and race, every language and group of the world (see Revelation 7:9).

As the friends of Jesus, we can experience fellowship with others in God's adopted family here and now. As we mutually recognize Jesus as our common Friend, our present fellowship together will take on special qualities that will reflect what our adopted family in heaven will be like. It will be an encouraging community in heaven, and so it should be here. God teaches us, "In response to all he has done for us, let us outdo each other in being helpful and kind to each other and in doing good. Let us not neglect our church meetings, as some people do, but encourage and warn each other, especially now that the day of his coming back is drawing near" (Hebrews 10:24,25 TLB).

The Marks of Genuine Friendship

Jesus desires that His family in local churches be caring friends. He said, "By this all will know that you are My disciples, if you have love for one another" (John 13:35). He also taught "Love one another; as I have loved you" (John 13:34). While we were still helpless, ungodly sinners, Christ loved us enough to die for us (see Romans 5:6–8). One outstanding mark of God's family members is that we genuinely care for one another and show it in tangible ways.

Genuine fellowship is marked by the desire to share God-given material possessions with one another. This may be meals (see Acts 2:46), it may be a bed, it may be the opportunity to obtain a job for a fellow Christian who is out of work. Sharing may mean helping someone financially. It may mean sharing spiritual gifts and talents with one another.

Fellowship means that friends of Jesus learn to depend on one another. Just like the parts of the body depend on one another to keep the body as a whole alive, so Jesus' friends depend on one another.

Mutual dependency leads us to mutual service. Fellowship means being at the disposal of one another and showing an unceasing interest in one another. The Bible reminds us in Philippians 2:4 to "let each of you look out not only for his own interests, but also for the interests of others."

Fellowship means that we love one another. Because we love one another, we will devote ourselves to prayer for one another. We will intercede for the needs of others to be met. We will also pray for God's desires to come to pass on this earth (see Acts 1:14).

Fellowship promotes prayer even as prayer strengthens and motivates our fellowship. When we pray for those with whom we fellowship, we reap benefits in at least two ways: We become closer to the Lord, and He cultivates within us a deep love for our fellow Christians and non-Christians in our midst.

True fellowship is also marked by a desire to learn about the One who has brought His friends together as a family (see Acts 20:7). When we get together, we want to learn more about Jesus and what He has done. We can never learn enough about the One we love.

The by-product of true fellowship is unity. "Now the multitude of those who believed were one heart and one soul" (Acts 4:32). Fellowship in one word is *sharing.* Where genuine sharing with one another occurs, unity of spirit will be the result.

What Will Damage Fellowship

Genuine fellowship is exciting, but it is also fragile because it can be easily damaged. *It is damaged by sin.* Therefore as friends of Jesus, we cannot afford to allow opportunity for sin in our lives. If we are compromising and practicing known sin, then fellowship with Jesus and His friends is damaged. "If we say that we have fellowship with Him, and walk in darkness, we lie and do not practice the truth. But if we walk in the light as He is in the light, we have fellowship with one another, and the blood of Jesus Christ His Son cleanses us from all sin" (1 John 1:6–7).

If there is a known sin you are having difficulty in overcoming, then ask God to give you someone with whom you can be open and honest. Do not attempt to tackle the problem in your own power or by yourself. But do attempt to deal with it, rather than let it choke out your relationship with Jesus and others.

The best way to develop the local church as a community of caring friends is for each of us to concentrate on being close to Jesus. We should keep our eyes on Jesus, even in church. If we compare ourselves improperly to others in church, it is easy to get discouraged. At times others are not what they should be. At other times they appear to be so far ahead of us in their spiritual lives that we may fear we will never catch up. Like spokes on a wheel that get closer to each other as they are nearer to the hub, believers who are near to Christ will be closer to one another. Together with them we will have more ability to properly relate to professing Christians who are distant from Christ. We also will increasingly be able to minister to those who are not in God's family.

Fellowship is a lifestyle, not just a church activity. Fellowship is not limited to a specific time, place, or form. It is an expression of our relationship with Jesus who is with us at all times. Therefore, fellowship may be enjoyed any hour of the day or night. Any place where we meet and share in one another's lives, there is fellowship. Fellowship cannot be separated from the events of ordinary life, for we share them with others who are Jesus' friends.

Forgiveness

Fellowship with Jesus and His friends is possible because we have a new relationship based on Christ's forgiveness of our sins. Jesus desires that our fellowship also be marked by a willingness to forgive one another. We are not to be a family marred by grudges and backbiting. Jesus says we are to bury the hatchet and forgive one another. Jesus forgave Peter when he denied Him and fled. He forgave Thomas when he doubted. He forgave James and John when pride caused them to argue over who would be greatest in the kingdom of heaven. And He tells us, "Love one another; as I have loved you." This is a voluntary, self-sacrificing love. It is love that is given even when the person being loved is not lovable. When Jesus gave the model prayer to His disciples, He included the forgiveness of others when He taught, "Forgive us our debts, as we forgive our debtors" (Matthew 6:12).

God indicates that a concrete way of expressing love to Himself and others is to extend forgiveness to those who have offended you. He says,

> You shall not hate your brother in your heart....You shall not take vengeance, nor bear any grudge...but you shall love your neighbor as yourself: I am the LORD (Leviticus 19:17–18).

When wronged, your nature says to retaliate. The Bible teaches, "Repay no one evil for evil" (Romans 12:17). Instead, "receive one another, just as Christ also received us, to the glory of God" (Romans 15:7). As your Friend, Jesus will help you relate in a constructive manner to those who have offended you.

Properly Applying Forgiveness

The concept of forgiveness can be applied in a misunderstood way, however. If it is, you run the risk of becoming a doormat to others' abuses.

Tim became careless about his actions at work. His work often was shoddy, and he did not complete his assignments on time. He believed that if he simply said, "I'm sorry," to his boss, all of his wrong behavior was immediately forgiven and forgotten. He continued this pattern until his boss drew the line and let him know that unless there was immediate change in his performance it would be his last week at his company. Tim realized his words would no longer be sufficient. There would have to be a change in behavior.

Forgiveness must be applied with tough love. Easy forgiveness will not do. At times love dictates that you lovingly confront the offender. "Don't hate your brother. Rebuke anyone who sins; don't let him get away with it, or you will be equally guilty" (Leviticus 19:17 TLB).

It is too easy to succumb to what feels like Christian peer pressure that says, "It is wrong to be upset. Just forgive him and bind your wounds in private." If angry or resentful feelings between conflicting parties are not dealt with, those feelings will fester. Left untreated, they will destroy or at least hamper the vitality and love of the individuals and their surrounding community. Stuffing a devisive issue is not love.

Genuine love is built on the foundation of respect and accountability, which are necessary in every relationship. To maintain them, you need to confront an offender who is taking advantage of you rather than extend easy forgiveness. This is for *his* ultimate benefit.

For *your* benefit and for the sake of the new friendship you now have with Jesus, you must forgive the offender from your heart whether he acknowledges wrongdoing or not. Do not give Satan a foot in the door of your life by holding a grudge.

"I need a college degree in engineering to figure this out," mumbled Sam as he tried desperately to assemble his son's new bicycle. EASY ASSEMBLY was blazoned across the box, and under these words were included, ANY AMATEUR CAN PUT THIS BICYCLE TOGETHER IN A FEW MINUTES. Sam had been working on the project for hours. His problem was that he hadn't read the instruction book first. If he had followed the proper step-by-step procedure, he could have completed the task quickly. God has given us His instructions for maintaining relationships, and he has offered forgiveness as the key to their success. We need to read His instructions, however, in order to know how to apply that forgiveness in a relationship. If we don't extend forgiveness, there will be much frustration.

Properly extending forgiveness means several things. First, it means taking the initiative. As a Christian, you must not wait until others come to you and ask to be forgiven (see Matthew 18:15). Remember, forgiveness is the key that unlocks the door of resentment and the handcuffs of hate. It is a power that breaks the chains of bitterness and the shackles of selfishness.

You have been forgiven by God to whom you were deeply indebted (see Matthew 18:23–35). He in turn expects you to forgive others freely because of the forgiveness you have experienced. The degree to which you realize the reality of your own forgiveness is expressed by how quickly you grant others forgiveness. God took the initiative to forgive you, so you need to reach out in forgiveness to those who offend you.

Second, extending forgiveness means developing selective amnesia (see Jeremiah 31:34). When you forgive someone, you need to *act* as if you have forgotten the offense and treat the offender as forgiven.

A prominent man was asked by a reporter if he remembered an incident in which a friend had hurt him deeply. He quickly replied, "No, I specifically remember forgetting it." Not only has God forgiven your sins, but He has forgotten them as well. He will not dig the incident up once He has forgiven it. He buries it in the deepest ocean (see Micah 7:19) and puts up a sign that says: NO FISHING. This is a good discipline too for you to develop.

Third, the act of forgiveness often will cost the one who forgives (see Luke 23:34). In order to forgive us, God had to sacrifice His only Son who took the penalty for our sins. In order for you to forgive someone, you may have to sacrifice your pride, your reputation, your money, or your rights.

The Power of Forgiveness

Forgiveness is powerful. It can transform people. King David spoke of a time when he experienced a sense of deep guilt. He had committed adultery and murder and then attempted to cover them up, but the weight of these acts crushed him. He knew he had offended God and others. He said, "When I kept silent, my bones grew old. My vitality was turned into the drought of summer" (Psalm 32:3–4). In contrast, when David confessed his sins and received forgiveness, he was a freed man. He exclaimed,

> Blessed is he whose transgression is forgiven,
> Whose sin is covered....
> I said, "I will confess my transgressions to the LORD,"
> And You forgave the iniquity of my sin (Psalm 32:1,5).

Forgiving those who offend us is a concrete means of showing love to God and others and preserving fellowship at its best. If we live in the atmosphere and attitude of forgiveness toward all, we will find our love for God branching out in other ways. We will have a desire to serve others. Let's examine what that gift of service looks like.

Reflections

1. What do I understand this to be saying?

2. What is God telling me to do that I'm not afraid to do?

3. What do I want to understand better?

4. What is God telling me that I find hard to apply to my life?

10

No Hands but Yours

10   Service

*C*ontrary to what today's society advocates, the Bible teaches that if you want great riches, you must give away; that the way up is down; and that if you would be great, you must become a servant or slave to Jesus Christ and His followers.

Jesus took the form of a servant when He washed the disciples' feet at His Last Supper. He taught that whoever would be exalted must first be abased. Are you willing to humble yourself in the role of a servant as an expression of love to God?

If our goal is to discover how we can grow in a close intimate, personal relationship with Jesus, how do we do it? How do we grow to intimately know Someone who we cannot visibly see, physically touch, or audibly hear? How do we express love to such a Friend? Jesus answered these questions for us when He said, "If you love Me, keep My commandments" (John 14:15). Loving obedience is how we express our love to Jesus.

An important means of expressing our love to God is

through serving one another. As we consider this particular facet of love, let's briefly focus on four questions that will help us direct our thoughts:

1. What do I understand this to be saying?
2. What is God telling me to do that I'm not afraid to try?
3. What do I want to understand better?
4. What is God telling me that I find hard to apply to my life?

Servanthood

God tells us in Galatians 5:13–14, "Through love serve one another." The entire law is summed up in a single commandment: "Love your neighbor as yourself." Service then is an opportunity to directly express love to others and ultimately to God. Service is also the ingredient that holds our fellowship together. As we look for opportunities to meet the needs of others, the friends of Jesus grow closer together.

Historically, in our culture, those who serve others have been viewed as low men on the totem pole. Service has typically had an unpopular, distasteful connotation. The servant has been associated with the days of slavery and lowly occupations. A slave was perceived as one who worked out of compulsion or duty with little freedom to fulfill personal desires. Very few of us have a positive picture of a servant, much less aspire to be a servant. The lack of freedom and the lowly task strike us as distasteful.

The New Testament model of service originated from a very special kind of servant called a "love servant." The love servant was one who, after faithful service, was offered his freedom by his master. However, because of his special affection for his master, and as an expression of love, he instead chose to remain a slave. The master was required to mark his special love servant by placing the servant's earlobe against a doorpost and driving an awl through it. The love servant offered his service from a heart of love rather than compulsion or obligation (see Exodus 21:5,6). As the friends of Jesus, we are to offer our services to others as an expression of our love to Jesus.

Jesus asked His disciple, Simon Peter, the question, "Simon, son of Jonah, do you love Me more than these?" Peter responded, "Yes, Lord; You know that I love You." Jesus said then, "Feed My lambs" (John 21:15). By that He meant, "Meet the needs of My friends." As our Friend, Jesus is requesting the same of us. Our bodies and spiritual gifts are the tools we use to serve others. The unique gifts and abilities He has entrusted to us are for the purpose of meeting the needs of others. One day when we stand before God, He will require an accounting of how we have used our gifts. We can selfishly choose to use them for our own advantage, or we can choose to employ them for the advantage of others.

The apostle Paul pleaded,

And so, dear brothers, I plead with you to give your bodies to God. Let them be a living sacrifice, holy—the kind he can accept. When you think of what He has done for you, is this too much to ask? (Romans 12:1 TLB).

Serving God's Family

The Church is often compared to the human body.

This body has many "members" just as the human body does. Each member receives from and gives to other members. As an arm receives from the shoulder and gives to the hand, so the members of Christ's body also receive and give to one another. Scripture explains, "But now God has set the members, each one of them in the body just as He pleased" (1 Corinthians 12:18).

Christ wants you attached to His body in a local church. The person who says he trusts Christ but does not need the church is like a hand severed from the arm saying it does not need to be attached. The severed hand cannot live long separated from the body. Neither can the isolated Christian grow if he is separated from the community of Jesus' friends. Scripture urges, "Let us not neglect our church meetings, as some people do, but encourage and warn each other, especially now that the day of His coming back again is drawing near" (Hebrews 10:25 TLB).

Giving and Receiving

Just as a healthy body needs intake and output to remain healthy, so too a healthy member of a local church must receive from and give to other members. With a proper balance of intake and output, you will grow increasingly stronger. Remember, your physical body needs adequate food, rest, and exercise to grow. The Church as the body of Christ also needs a proper balance of intake and output if it is to grow stronger. In turn, as you grow stronger, you can use your strength to do God's will. Every part of the body should be at maximum strength, available for God's use at all times.

In doing His will you will gain skill and confidence to

do still more. None of Jesus' friends is purely ornamental. Each has a specific, useful function. Any person who can be content doing nothing in and through the local church may not be a part of the "church of the firstborn who are registered in heaven" (Hebrews 12:23).

Accountability

Jesus doesn't intend for any of His friends to be merely bench warmers. *He intends for you as His friend to use the talents He gives you.* No one is exempt! Scripture says, "As each one has received a gift, minister it to one another, as good stewards of the manifold grace of God" (1 Peter 4:10). One day Jesus will ask how you have used the natural abilities, talents, and gifts He has given you.

Jesus described this moment in a brief story. A certain rich man gave his servants some money to invest. Later he asked for an accounting. The majority of the servants invested the money, but one servant did not. He foolishly "dug in the ground, and hid his lord's money" (Matthew 25:18). The rich man took his money back and called this servant "wicked and lazy" (Matthew 25:26). God expects you to exercise faith as His friend and to use all the abilities you have as avenues to serve Him.

The Mark of Genuine Love

Love will always serve. When Amy was asked at the last minute to host a women's meeting at her home, she knew it would take several hours to get the house ready for eighteen women. Her husband, Rob, saw her dilemma and pitched in to help. Of course, he did several things wrong, and there were a few heated words from exasperated Amy; but together they were able to put things in order because of their love for each other and their desire to be of service to others.

If you love others, you will risk danger. You will get dirty. You will assume responsibility. You will care in tangible, practical ways. The original meaning of *to serve* in Latin means "to give oneself trouble." No better phrase can describe what it means to serve others, for loving service will entail a cost. Jesus Himself served others to the point of sacrificially offering His own life.

Mark 10:45 tells us, "For even the Son of Man did not come to be served, but to serve, and to give His life a ransom for many." Jesus continually served the needy. He healed the sick, opened the eyes of the blind, made the lame whole, fed the hungry. In fact, Jesus so identifies with the needy that He considers our acts of kindness to them as though they were done directly to Him. He explained:

> When the Son of Man comes in His glory, and all the holy angels with Him, then He will sit on the throne of His glory. All the nations will be gathered before Him, and He will separate them one from another, as a shepherd divides his sheep from the goats. And He will set the sheep on His right hand, but the goats on the left. Then the King will say to those on His right hand, "Come, you blessed of My Father; inherit the kingdom prepared for you from the foundation of the world: for *I was hungry and you gave Me food; I was thirsty and you gave Me drink; I was a stranger and you took Me in; I was naked and you clothed Me; I was sick and you visited Me; I was in prison and you came to Me.*" Then the righteous will answer Him, saying, "Lord, when did we see You hungry and feed You, or thirsty and give You drink? When did we see You a stranger and take You in, or naked and clothe You? Or when did we see You sick, or in prison, and come to You?" And the King will answer and

say to them, "Assuredly, I say to you inasmuch as you did it to one of the least of these My brethren, you did it to me" (Matthew 25:31–40, italics added).

Serving our neighbors and serving Christ are the same thing. In Europe, before an old cathedral stands a statue of Christ with His arms outstretched. During World War II the cathedral was bombed, and the hands of the statue were blown off. After the war, the cathedral was rebuilt, but the statue was left unchanged. Instead, a sign was hung at its base that read, "Christ has no hands but yours." Jesus desires our hands to do His work in others' lives. He asks to use our hands to serve those in need.

Serving with the Best

In most areas of service there may be a wide difference between the "good" and the "best." While kitchen duty for church functions may be a good service for Judy, her real gift is teaching. On the other hand, Mary is an excellent cook and could best serve in the kitchen, not as a teacher in Sunday school. We need to learn to distinguish between the good and the best.

God's work done His way and in His time always brings fulfillment in your heart. As you consciously choose to obey His desires, you will notice that part of the fulfillment He gives is a positive self-image. As you continue to obey Him in the various realms of your life, your sense of self-worth and fulfillment will increase as a by-product. God always provides enough time, energy, and ability to do His whole will. The key question you must constantly ask is, What is His will? Usually you will have no difficulty telling the bad from the good in your decision-making process. The biggest challenge is distinguishing the good from the best. Only as you stay close to Jesus will you be able to know and choose the best.

Discernment is required in choosing the best means of serving others. Sometimes well-meaning fellow members of God's family will urge you to do things they feel are important. This *may* be God's way of showing you His will. However, on occasion you will be pressed to do things that appear good, maybe even necessary, but they are not God's *best* for you. It is possible for you to succeed in a task that is not God's will, and as a result you may feel empty or even arrogant. Failure to do God's best will ultimately frustrate you. Doing His will is fulfilling and rewarding.

Trying to do things that are less than God's best or attempting to do too many things will turn your efforts into toil and drudgery. This may occur even when the things you choose appear good and necessary.

This is illustrated in a story concerning a community of woodland animals. They all decided they needed to become more versatile. A curriculum was chosen that required everyone to master the activities of running, jumping, swimming, and flying. There was enthusiastic support for the program. However, the program quickly hit several snags. The eagle, who was a fantastic flier, performed pitifully as a runner. The turtle, who was a superb swimmer, couldn't pass jumping. The frog, a learned leaper, flunked flying. The deer, a regal runner, had to be pulled from the pond during swimming class. The animals found they spent so much time focusing on their weak events that their strong areas soon atrophied. The activities they were trying to master were good, but they were not the best that God had enabled them to do. They became frustrated and discouraged.

There is a lesson to be learned from this story. Simply put, its moral is "choose that which God enables you to do well." He wants to use your abilities for His great purposes. His purposes are fulfilling. Focus on these. God wants you to work for Him. In the process He will use the work you choose to shape you into the likeness of Jesus.

God has prepared certain individuals in your local church to help you develop your gifts and abilities. They are there "for the equipping of the saints for the work of ministry" (Ephesians 4:12). Consult with your pastor or teachers as to how you can best develop your gifts and abilities into ministries of service in your local church. They will help guide you in your desire to choose God's best.

Loving obedience is rewarding. Probably no other facet of loving God is more immediately rewarding than sharing the best news about your Best Friend with another individual. In our next chapter, we will focus on expressing our love for God by telling our friends about our intimate relationship with Him.

Reflections

1. What do I understand this to be saying?

2. What is God telling me to do that I'm not afraid to try?

3. What do I want to understand better?

4. What is God telling me that I find hard to apply to my life?

11

The Friendly Witness

11   **Witnessing**

*J*ames Hudson Taylor, a missionary to China, was
traveling on a river one day when he spotted a
small capsized boat. A single passenger had been
aboard it. He quickly rowed over to the spot to help the
man but saw no sign of him. Diving several times, he
had no success. Calling to a nearby fishing boat, he
screamed, "Come quickly! A man is drowning here!
Bring your nets and help me!"

The fishermen replied, "We're too busy right now."

Taylor pleaded, "I'll pay you if you 'll just come now!"

"How much?" was their response.

"I'll give you ten dollars, but come now!"

"That's not enough," they said.

"Fifteen dollars is all I have! Please come quickly!"
he yelled.

Reluctantly the fishermen agreed to help. Slowly
they rowed their boat over to the spot where Taylor had
last seen the man. They lowered their nets and within
moments had located the man. As they pulled him to

the surface and into the boat, Taylor saw that he was dead. He had drowned while the fishermen haggled over money.

Right now, what do you feel after reading this story? You probably feel deep anger. How could the fishermen be so uncaring and indifferent? Why were they more concerned about the money than the drowning man? Certainly, if you had been there, you would have rushed to help.

However, before we are quick to judge, perhaps we ought to stop and consider. At times we may be just as indifferent as the fishermen. We may not be as callous at the scene of an accident, but in other ways we may be more like the fishermen than we realize.

Around us in our neighborhoods, in our jobs, and even in our own families are people who are drowning. They are drowning in their sins, separated from an intimate, personal relationship with God. They may feel isolated and carry heavy burdens. Oftentimes they may feel overwhelmed by guilt and anxiety. Deep down, they may feel purposeless in life.

You have the opportunity to encourage them with the best news. You can tell them there is Someone who cares and wants to be their intimate Friend. You have the solution that they need to hear, the solution that you looked to find for such a long time. Now that you know Jesus as your Best Friend, others need to know what you possess in Christ and how you came to possess it. When you love your neighbor as yourself, you will want him also to have eternal life—a close personal relationship with the one true God and Jesus Christ whom He sent (see John 17:3). Your neighbor may not realize it, but a close personal relationship with God is exactly what he needs. Pascal wisely observed that every person has a God-shaped vacuum in his life, and no one can know fulfillment until that vacuum is filled with a personal relationship through His Son, Jesus.

Jesus said, "But you shall receive power when the Holy Spirit has come upon you; and you shall be witnesses to Me in Jerusalem, and in all Judea and Samaria, and to the end of the earth" (Acts 1:8). Being touched by Jesus places you in the service of witness. You need to pass the message that changes lives on to others. Jesus will give you the strength and courage to take this step.

Expectations

Ask God to show you the people with whom He wants you to share Christ. As you pray, visualize His Spirit moving over your neighborhood and stopping over the homes He wants to develop friendships with. Befriend those people. Pray for them, expecting God to work in their lives. Discover their interests and pursue those you find you have in common. You may enjoy playing tennis or going to a social event together. As you develop the relationship, let them see and hear what knowing Christ as your Best Friend has meant in your life. Perhaps you already have several friends who do not know Jesus as their Best Friend. You can share your friendship with Jesus with them. The important thing is your attitude. Expect God to move in your neighborhood, your family, your job, your friends. Expect God to provide opportunities for you to share your experience with Jesus and to help others have that experience as well.

The Benefits of Sharing Christ

As you share Him with others, He will strengthen your awareness of eternal life. He promises, "Go-...make disciples...I am with you" (Matthew 28:19–20). Jesus makes His presence very real in a unique way when you lovingly obey His Great Commission. You experience greater intimacy with Him when you share Him with others.

As you allow God to show others how He "called you out of darkness into His marvelous light" (1 Peter 2:9), you will grow in your awareness of *what His grace has made you.* You are a son or a daughter of the King of the universe. You are holy and pure in His eyes. Before you knew Jesus, you were less than nothing. Now you are God's very own. You are only a visitor here. Your real home is in heaven.

Jesus is too big to keep to yourself! If you found a million dollars, could you keep quiet about it? Jesus as your Best Friend is far more valuable to you than a million dollars. That is how Peter and John felt. When they were ordered to stop talking about Jesus and threatened when they shared Jesus with others, they had a quick reply: "Whether it is right in the sight of God to listen to you more than to God, you judge. For we cannot but speak the things which we have seen and heard" (Acts 4:19–20).

Who Do I Talk With?

Who around you needs to know Jesus as an intimate Friend? Who do you know in need of a life with purpose? Who is looking for meaning beyond self? Who needs a full life to replace one that is withered and dried up from recent disappointment and difficulties? Who do you know in need of eternal life? Who among your friends needs to know Christ intimately? Do your neighbors living on either side of you need to know Jesus? Does someone at work need to know your Best Friend.

Through you, God wants to reach your family and friends.* They cannot call upon Him in whom they have not believed. They cannot believe in Him whom they have not heard, for "faith comes by hearing, and hearing by the word of God" (Romans 10:14–17).

Jesus wants you to share the best news you have ever heard that someone initially shared with you. You must pass on to others what you have received from Christ, namely, news of a new, intimate relationship with God that grows through faith and loving obedience. To tell the best news is simply to express what you possess in Christ and to explain how you came to possess it.

Our Motivation to Speak Out

Pretend you are a research scientist. In your lab one day after years and years of failure, you discover a cure for cancer. What would you do? Would you hide it? Would you keep it to yourself? Of course not! You would want to share what you found with the millions today who are afflicted with cancer.

All people are afflicted with the cancer of sin. Sin, like untreated cancer, produces death. Sin, however,

*If you need help in determining which of your friends might be open to the gospel, do a relationship review. How to do this is explained in the booklet *Relationship Review, How to be a Friend for Life*, available from your local bookstore or by writing Serve International, P. O. Box 723846, Atlanta, GA 30339.

produces eternal death—everlasting separation from the one true God (see Romans 5:12). Jesus, through His life, death, and resurrection, is the cure. When you believe this and care for others, you will seek to share Jesus with them. The news you have concerning the intimate relationship you have with Jesus as your Best Friend is just as exciting as news about a newfound cure for cancer!

How to Speak Out

How you share the news of your Best Friend is as important as what you share. If anyone is offended when you share, be sure the cause for offense is the message of the gospel and not you. When you love God and your neighbor, you will want to do what pleases God and is for the good of your neighbor. Therefore, you will always want to speak the truth in love (see Ephesians 4:15). Love without truth is empty sentiment and emotion. Truth without love is harsh and abrasive. Jesus said, "For out of the abundance of the heart the mouth speaks" (Matthew 12:34). When you speak the truth in love, you demonstrate that your heart is in tune with God. Your neighbor will take note and be more inclined to listen if you keep this simple rule of thumb in mind.

Witnessing to your neighbors, friends, and relatives about the friendship you have with Jesus and the impact that friendship has had on your life is a means of saying thank you to Jesus. It is a concrete way of expressing your love to Him and showing genuine concern for your friends who do not yet know Him as their Best Friend.**

As you express your love to God by speaking to your friends about Him, be aware that you will encounter hindrances designed to stop you. Our next chapter is to acquaint you with the source of these hindrances and your new enemy.

**Some find it helpful to give a brief printed presentation of the gospel to their friends and then to discuss it. The *Best News* is a 32-page booklet containing an illustrated presentation of the gospel. It can be obtained from your local bookstore or by writing to Serve International, P. O. Box 723846, Atlanta, GA 30339. Serve International also provides materials and seminars for helping you to share the Gospel with your friends in a conversational format. This course is called *Life Cycle Relational Evangelism Training*.

Reflections

1. What do I understand this to be saying?

2. What is God telling me to do that I'm not afraid to do?

3. What do I want to understand better?

4. What is God telling me that I find hard to apply to my life?

PART IV

Overcoming Obstacles to Your Friendship with God

12

The Enemy Without

---

12   Satan

*J*ust two months ago Hal made Jesus his Best
Friend. Recently, though, Hal has been wondering
what he got himself into. It seems that in the last week
everything has been going wrong with no reasonable
explanation. Just when he was beginning to be able to
talk more freely about his newfound Friend and the impact Jesus has had on his life, Hal became sick. He
hadn't been sick in years, but suddenly he was flat on
his back with a fever of 102°. As if that wasn't enough,
the boss informed him that the company's largest cli-
ent, who was Hal's responsibility, called to say his services would no longer be needed. The company got a
new boss who had "old friends" he preferred to do
business with. To top it off, Hal's car, which he always
parked on the street in front of his house, was side-
swiped by a hit-and-run driver last night. The damage
was at least $1,500 worth. Needless to say, Hal was dis-
couraged. He picked up the phone and called Frank.
Frank had shared the *Best News* booklet with him and

had discussed how he could have a personal relationship with Jesus.

"Frank, this is Hal."

"Hal! How are you doing?"

"Not too good," replied Hal, and he went on to describe all that had happened to him in the last week. "Frank, I'm pretty discouraged. What's happening? All these things are happening to me with no reasonable explanation. I'm trying to show my love to Jesus, and it seems so much is going wrong lately."

There was a brief pause before Frank answered. "Hal, it sounds to me like the Enemy is making you a special target of his attacks."

"The Enemy?" asked Hal.

"Yes," said Frank, "you may not remember, Hal, but I warned you about him that night you prayed to ask Jesus to take control of your life. I said, 'Hal, now that you've asked Jesus to be your Best Friend, you have a new enemy. Satan is his name. He is your enemy because he is the archenemy of Jesus. Now that you've identified yourself with Jesus, he is going to attack you and try to drive doubt and discouragement into your relationship with Jesus.' It sounds like that is exactly what he's up to now."

"But I thought Satan was just a fictitious character with horns, a tail, and red tights that someone made up. You mean to tell me he's for real, Frank?"

"Yes, Hal, he is," Frank replied. "Satan himself wants people to be skeptical of his existence. That way he can be more effective. If you doubt he exists, then he can do his work undetected."

"I never thought of that," Hal replied.

"Jesus believed in the reality of Satan," Frank added.

"In fact He had more to say about Satan than anyone else in the Bible. Jesus had no doubt about his reality." Frank continued, "Satan can also take on various disguises, Hal. To Eve in the Garden of Eden, he appeared in the form of a clever serpent. In the New Testament, he is described as presenting himself seductively as an 'angel of light' (2 Corinthians 11:14). He knows he is more likely to accomplish his plans if he appears in a captivating and alluring form."

Frank had Hal's attention by now. Hal wanted to know more about his Enemy. After all, he was experiencing him firsthand these days.

"Tell me, Frank. What is Satan's goal? Why is he bothering me? I don't consider myself much of a threat to him, so why is he attacking me right now?"

"Well, Hal, it's nothing personal. You see, Jesus is Satan's enemy, but Jesus is too powerful for Satan to directly attack Him. Therefore, Satan goes after those persons who are the closest and mean the most to Jesus, but who are vulnerable, namely, you. His favorite targets are the friends of Jesus. His goal is to try to destroy them anyway he can. He knows he can indirectly get at Jesus through hurting His friends. That's why he is attacking you right now. Especially since you've started talking to your friends about Jesus."

"He doesn't sound like a nice guy!" Hal joked. "But tell me, Frank, just how powerful is Satan? I mean if he is able to attack my health, my business, and my possessions, that has me worried."

Frank responded, "That's a good question, Hal. Actually none of us is a match for a foe of his cunning, intelligence, power, and hatred. Satan can deceive us. He can overcome us. He could even murder us. Left to our own resources, we would not have a hope. Fortunately, though his power is great, he is limited by God's power. He is ultimately subject to God's authority and can do no more than God allows him to.

"As you've experienced, Hal, Satan can attack our health and our possessions. But his primary point of attack seems to be our minds. The discouragement you mentioned is his favorite tool to put a wedge between you and the Lord. The experiences you're having are only a first wave of attack. The second wave of attack, discouragement, is the tool Satan hopes will overcome you. He hopes the discouragement will produce doubts in your mind about the genuineness of your relationship with Jesus.

"Jesus warned His friends of Satan's tactic when He said, 'then the devil comes and takes away the word out of their hearts, lest they should believe and be saved' (Luke 8:12). Hal, Satan is attempting to spoil your friendship with Jesus. He wants you to believe that if you really were Jesus' friend, Jesus wouldn't allow these things to happen to you. Be on your guard. Satan is playing mind games with you."

Hal thought for a moment about what Frank had just said. What Frank had observed was exactly what was happening in his life. Satan was using these events to try and drive a wedge between him and Jesus.

"Frank, I have another question. You said Satan likes to drive a wedge between the Lord and me by using discouraging circumstances. Are there other tools that Satan likes to use to discourage my relationship with Jesus?"

"Well, Hal, Satan has a whole arsenal of weapons he can and does use. Besides discouragement, there are doubt, depression, and disaster which you are well acquainted with. He can also use fear and pride. Guilt is another effective tool Satan has found. No Christian has to be very old in the faith before he realizes that he has not attained absolute perfection. The devil constantly assaults us at this point by saying, 'You're not good enough…you're not good enough yet. God doesn't have total, absolute, 100 percent control of your life. Who do you think you are, talking to someone else about Him?' If you haven't experienced that one yet, you can expect it, Hal. Satan is the 'accuser of our brethren' (Revelation 12:10).

"Sometimes it can be difficult to tell the difference between the true conviction of the Holy Spirit and the false accusations of the devil, Hal. Jesus said that the Holy Spirit would 'convict the world of sin' (John 16:8). When the Holy Spirit convicts, He deals with specific things that are present realities. He seeks to bring us to repentance and faith so that our lives may be strengthened. The devil comes with a counterfeit conviction. He reminds us of sins already confessed and forgiven. He deals in vague generalities and feelings of inadequacy. All this he does to cripple you and me as Christians.

"Probably the easiest tool for Satan to use, though, is temptation."

"Ah, temptation, " Hal interrupted in a knowing tone of voice. "I've had a rough time handling that one throughout my whole life, but I seem to be more aware of it since I've known Jesus. Do you ever have problems with it, Frank?"

"I certainly do!" said Frank. "Though not all temptation comes directly from Satan. Sometimes it comes from our own desires. Satan will use any avenue of opportunity to lead us away. Hal, I have discovered Satan can particularly use sins I struggled with before I was a Christian to trip up my relationship with Jesus. I used to lie without blinking an eye before I came into a friendship with Jesus. If it was advantageous, I didn't have a problem doing it. But since I've known Jesus, I've discovered that one of the things He says that demonstrates love for Him is refraining from lying. Now, I find I struggle most with this temptation when I'm placed in a situation where a lie would make me look better for the moment than the truth would. It's a struggle every time, but I find the more I choose what's right, the easier it becomes. I find the more I choose the wrong, the easier it becomes as well. Temptation becomes harder to combat the more I give in to it."

"So how do you overcome it, Frank?" Hal asked.

Frank paused thoughtfully. "I find the use of Scripture in temptation is a powerful weapon, Hal. The devil is not afraid of me, but he is afraid of what God speaks. To overcome temptation regularly, I find I need to learn God's Word by heart and use it with confidence when Satan attacks. I also find that avoiding situations in which I know I'll be tempted is helpful. A verse that has helped me the most during times of temptation says, 'For in that He Himself has suffered, being tempted, He is able to aid those who are tempted' (Hebrews 2:18).

"Hal, Jesus is a Friend who helps us rather than runs from us when temptation comes. Don't feel guilty when you're tempted. Jesus Himself was tempted (see Hebrews 4:15). It's not the fact of temptation but the giving in to it that is wrong."

"I was wondering about that," Hal commented. "I'm

also wondering why God allows Satan to tempt me. I mean if He is more powerful than Satan and if He is my Friend, why does He permit Satan to pressure me in this way?"

"That's a good question, Hal. I wondered about that a long time myself. Then someone shared with me that God loves us enough to want us to grow. He doesn't smother us. When God allows pressures to come on us, He wants us to overcome them with His help and become stronger. So there is a good purpose behind struggles. They help us grow in character. However, when Satan brings temptations and struggle, he wants to use those very same pressures to overwhelm us and to weaken us afterward. God can use Satan's tactics for good ends, though, even temptation.

"Hal, there's one last thing I think is important to remember in this attack you're going through right now. It might help to encourage you."

"I could sure use some encouragement right now." Hal sighed. "Please tell me!"

"The Scriptures encourage us when we read, 'He who is in you, is greater than he who is in the world' (1 John 4:4). One of the most exciting parts of being Jesus' friend is that we share in the victory that Christ had over Satan on the cross. Jesus now lives within you and me by His Spirit; therefore, you and I can do everything through Him who gives us strength (see Philippians 4:13). Hal, Satan is a defeated foe. His ultimate outcome is not in doubt. Therefore, you need not be afraid of Satan and his attacks. As long as you trust Jesus and are obedient to His desires, you can depend on His Spirit and confidently rebuke Satan's attacks and discouragements in your life. That's the encouraging news! We already have the final victory over Satan.

"So," Frank continued, "don't allow these present discouragements to put a wedge between you and Jesus—that's exactly what Satan wants.

"What's your favorite dessert, Hal?" Frank asked.

"Carrot cake," replied Hal, "but why do you ask?"

"Well, there's an old saying, 'Starve a cold and feed a fever.' I thought I might fatten you up and get you back on your feet! I'll pick up a carrot cake and drop by to see you tonight at 7:30. We can talk further if you want to."

"Thanks, Frank, you're a great friend. I'll look forward to seeing you then."

Reflections

1. What do I understand this to be saying?

2. What is God telling me to do that I'm not afraid to do?

3. What do I want to understand better?

4. What is God telling me that I find hard to apply to my life?

13

The Enemy Within

13   Sin

*H*ow do you grow in your personal relationship with Jesus? That is the question that our study in Best Friends has attempted to answer. Now you understand some of the basics to enhance your friendship. Growing in this relationship is a lifetime process. Many exciting and rewarding opportunities are yet to come, but as in any relationship, it would be misleading to suggest there are only easy and good times ahead. Good relationships take shared experiences, time, and commitment to be rewarding. Before we consider the rewards of loving God, let's examine some hindrances to growth and intimacy you will experience in your friendship with Him. As you do so, consider four questions that will help you evaluate these ideas.

1. What do I understand this to be saying?
2. What is God telling me to do that I'm not afraid to try?
3. What do I want to understand better?

4. What is God telling me that I find hard to apply to my life?

Hindrances to Intimacy with God

There is one thing that God tells us blocks our sense of His presence in our lives. He says, "Your iniquities have separated you from your God" (Isaiah 59:2). Iniquities or "sins" separate us from intimacy with God.

Have you ever watched a woodsman at work splitting a large tree for firewood? The steel wedge is first started in the bark of the fallen tree. With every blow of the heavy steel mallet, the wedge goes further and further into the tree. Little by little the huge tree, once strong and beautiful, is divided and split until it no longer resembles what it once was. Our intimacy with God can be separated by the wedge of sin. This raises a puzzling question we need to try to answer. What exactly is "sin"?

What Is Sin?

The best way to understand what sin is, is to picture an archery target. If you shoot an arrow at the target and miss it, you miss the mark. *To sin* means "to miss the mark or standard." When we sin, we miss the standard that God has desired for us. He tells us His standards in His Word. These are the standards we are to aim at with His help. Sin is not breaking our own standards of right and wrong (which we are able to rationalize at times). When we set our own standards, our tendency is to shoot the arrow and then draw the bull's-eye wherever the arrow lands. God's standard remains the same. It does not move. Sin, therefore, is missing the target of His perfect desires for us.

When Does Sin Occur?

We sin whenever we disobey God's desires for us. Typically this happens when we choose to satisfy our own desires in wrong ways. Harry heard about a new position in his office that would be filled soon. He and his co-worker George were the most likely candidates for the promotion, and Harry knew if he didn't act fast, George would probably be chosen. Rather than pray about the matter and let God direct in the decision, he began a smear campaign against George in an effort to make himself look better to his boss.

If Harry had let God take control, he may not have been promoted to the new position, but God would have something much better for him in the future. When we assert our desires and means against God's and when we try to live independently of Him, we sin.

The Practice of Sin

Sin in our lives blocks true intimacy with God. Does this mean that we have to live perfect lives to sense God's presence in our lives? Does this mean that if we tell a lie, cheat the tollbooth machine with a plug quarter, or are indifferent to our spouses, we can never have intimacy with God? The answer to that is yes and no. *No*, we don't have to live perfect lives to have intimacy with God. Jesus has already paid for our sins past, present, and future by His death for us on the cross. We are and always will be sinners saved by His grace. But being sinners and practicing sin are two different things. A drunk is a practicing alcoholic, but not all alcoholics are drunks. Believers are not to willfully, premeditatedly practice sin, although they are and always will be sinners. If there is sin, God, the Holy Spirit, will convict the heart so that we can confess our sins and He can forgive and purify us (see 1 John 1:9). Therefore, no, we don't have to be perfect to have a sense of God's presence in our lives. But, *yes*, we do need to avoid practicing known sin if we are to sense Him in our lives. If we make a practice of telling lies, putting plug quarters in the tollbooth machine on the way to work each morning, or are being indifferent to our spouses, then there will be a barrier between the Lord and us. Practicing known sins blocks intimacy with God.

Why Do We Sin So Easily?

Another question that comes to mind is, Why do we sin in the first place? Sometimes it seems that we fall into sin naturally. Why? Paul, a close friend of Jesus, wrestled with this very question. He said:

> I don't understand myself at all, for I really want to do what is right, but I can't. I do what I don't want to do—what I hate. I know perfectly well that what I am doing is wrong, and my bad conscience proves that I agree with these laws I am breaking. But I can't help myself, because I'm no longer doing it. It is sin inside me that is stronger than I am that makes me do these evil things. I know I am rotten through and through so far as my old sinful nature is concerned. No matter which way I turn I can't make myself do right. I want to but I can't. When I want to do good, I don't; and when I try not to do wrong, I do it anyway. Now if I am doing what I don't want to, it is plain where the trouble is: sin still has me in its evil grip (Romans 7:15–20 TLB).

We sin in the first place because it is our natural inclination to sin. It is already a part of us from the moment we are born to want to assert ourselves and have our own way. We don't have to teach a small infant to demand its own way; it is in its nature to do so. During the first weeks of a new baby's life, she could care less if her mother is tired and sleepy. When she is hungry or wet, she will demand attention through her high-pitched cries. If they are not answered immediately, she learns to scream louder and louder until she gets what she wants. As she grows older she simply learns to express her demands in new ways.

How Do We Overcome Sin?

How do we learn to obey God rather than obey the voice in us that says to do things our own way? Perhaps an African believer has best answered that.

One day a missionary was enabled to lead an African in a remote village to the Lord. The African headed home, promising to return in one week's time. Upon his return, the missionary asked him how his week had been. The African responded that it had been a challenging week. It seems that he had a great deal of internal conflict.

He said, "I feel like there are two big dogs fighting in me; good dog and bad dog. They are fighting all the time."

"Which one wins?" the missionary asked.

"The one I feed," the native replied.

All of us can identify with the African in our own struggle with sin. Within each of us are two dogs fighting for control of our lives—the good that seeks to love Jesus by obeying His desires, and the bad that seeks to satisfy our own desires in wrong ways. The one we feed is the one who will win.

The Effects of Sin

What are the effects of the willful practice of sin? In

addition to affecting the relationship with God, it also affects the relationship with other people. Jim knew his appetite for power and prestige was hindering his relationship with the Lord. Because of an inferiority complex resulting from his childhood days, he tried everything he could to gain control of every event. When he met a new person, the first thing he would ask himself was, *How can this person help me in achieving my goals?* It wasn't long until his new friends sensed that his friendship was superficial and that they were only being used by Jim for his own benefit.

It is very difficult for a Christian to bear witness to the saving power of Christ while he practices willful sin. The rebellion of his heart will short-circuit the heavenly power needed to communicate to the heart of the hearer. And the example of his life will lead the observer to wonder what is so great about a relationship with God when this person is no better off than anyone else.

Because of the old nature and the sin that adheres to our souls, we will always have an awareness of our iniquity. Some people describe this awareness as a "still, small voice" in their consciences that gently nudges them when they have sinned. Others can sense a red light that blinks in their minds or a red flag that is raised when they willfully disobey God and the principles of His Word.

Confession of Sin

The important thing is to keep short accounts with the Lord. Each night before you lay your head on your pillow, ask the Holy Spirit to show you anything in your life that is displeasing to Him. Then confess specific sins to God asking His forgiveness and claiming His cleansing.

Practicing sin as a way of life is like cuddling and kissing a poisonous rattlesnake. However, the more you obey God's commandments, the more able you are to realize the presence of your Friend. Remember, Jesus said, "He who has My commandments and keeps them, it is he who loves Me. And he who loves Me will be loved by My Father, and I will love him and manifest Myself to him" (John 14:21). This means you will know more about Him and gain a greater sensitivity to His presence as you choose to obey Him throughout your day.

Reflections

1. What do I understand this to be saying?

2. What is God telling me to do that I'm not afraid to do?

3. What do I want to understand better?

4. What is God telling me that I find hard to apply to my life?

The Last Word: Reaping the Rewards

*J*esus wants to be your Best Friend. He wants you to make Him your Best Friend. He desires for you to experience all that relationship can be. With each new expression of loving obedience to Jesus' words, He will reveal more of Himself to you. Your intimacy and closeness will increase. Your friendship will grow. The more your friendship grows, the more like Him you will become. The more like Him you are,

- The more you will experience the reward of inner joy and peace.
- The more you will love others as He loves you.
- The more satisfaction you will gain doing His will.
- The more you will enjoy using what you own for purposes He leads you to.
- The more you will be able to speak of the best news about your Best Friend.
- The more delight you will discover in serving the needs of others.

Appendix:
How Memory Works

Necessary Connections

*E*very time you remember something, you must join something you know with something that is new. These must be joined so that when you think of one you will also think of the other. Most people try to memorize material by repeating it over and over. This is the hard way. You may eventually make connections between the pieces of information you are trying to learn, but you have no control over the process. It is a subconscious connection.

On the other hand, it is possible to consciously control the connecting process. Then you know when, where, why, and how the two items are joined. In fact, you will be able to see pictures of the items and their connections.

Sound-Alike Picture Words

It is always easier to remember what can be seen rather than what can only be heard. Therefore, it is helpful to develop a way to picture all words. Some words are automatically visual. You have no trouble seeing a tiger, elephant, flower, automobile, or banana in your mind, do you? You know what they look like because you have seen them in pictures or real life. But other words are not automatically visual. What do you see in your mind when you think of the word *believe?* Since the word *believe* can't be pictured, how about this:

A bee on a leaf can easily be pictured. You just saw it. Now, bee-leaf sounds very much like *believe,* so bee-leaf will remind you of the word *believe.* And most important, you can now see a picture of the word *believe* because of the sound-alike picture word that was developed. This sound-alike picture word system can be used to help you see words for the learning of God's Word.

Symbol-Picture Words

Some words are easier to visualize through a symbol than through the sound-alike system. For example, Scripture speaks of God sitting on the throne of the universe. Therefore, a throne can be used as a symbol-picture for the word *God.* For the word *Jesus,* a cross may be used.

The pictures appear absurd, but their absurdity will

help you recall the words. The absurd and unusual are easier to recall than the normal.

The appearance of the pictures does not alter the inspired authority of the words. The pictures are like scaffolding used to build a house. Without the scaffolding, it is harder to build the house. Yet, once the house is built, the scaffolding is not necessary.

Jesus said that Scripture is truth (see John 17:17). He also declared, "And you shall know the truth, and the truth shall make you free" (John 8:32). The more you know the truth of God's Word, the more free you are to be and do what you ought.

If you are interested in this method of memorization, consult with someone who is involved in LifeCycle Training. This person can introduce you to this concept and work with you on specific passages. Better yet, get involved in the next LifeCycle Training opportunity and discover for yourself how you can learn Scripture and apply what you've learned as you share it with others.

Where Do You Go From Here?

*I*f this book has been helpful in developing your intimate relationship with God and you would like to develop this relationship even more, Serve International offers you a free devotional guide entitled, *Best Friends: How to Maintain Your Relationship with God.*

This devotional guide expands the twelve themes found in this *Best Friends* book. Daily Bible reading, inspirational insights, and suggested additional Christian literature are provided focused on these themes. To receive your free copy, write your name and address on the Business Reply Card found in this book and check the box next to the *Best Friends* Devotional Guide.

If the card has been removed, you may request your free copy of the *Best Friends Devotional Guide* by writing: Serve International, P. O. Box 723846, Atlanta, GA 30339.

What Is Serve International?

*S*erve International is an interdenominational equipping ministry. It provides materials and seminars for the process of congregational renewal, basic nurture of new believers, and relational evangelism training. It culminates in mobilization to full ministry through discovering and using one's spiritual gifts. This process dynamically blends Church Growth principles and sound educational principles. It is a cumulative curriculum that helps a new believer grow from profession of faith to the point of responsible evangelistic reproduction through their local church and provides an understanding of where one fits in the challenge of world evangelism. The end product of this process is a local church that is an equipping station for world evangelism and church members who are world class disciple makers.

Best Friends is the first course in this curriculum.

The royalties payable on the sales of this book and other Serve International printed materials have been assigned to expanding the ministry of Serve International which exists to help church leaders equip witness-builders to build the church to evangelize the world. Inquiries and donations should be sent to: Serve International, P.O. Box 723846, Atlanta, GA 30339.

How to Start a Best Friends Group

---

*W*hy not ask your friends to join you in a group where you can read and discuss this book together? You could draw from your friends at work or your neighbors. Maybe your friends at school or an exercise class would be interested in getting together to read *Best Friends* and discuss the ideas presented in each chapter. Closer to home, you may consider using *Best Friends* for your family devotions with your family members as your *Best Friends* Group. If you are involved in a local church, you might like to form a Bible study group or a Sunday School class using *Best Friends* as your text.

You can use the "Reflection" questions at the end of each chapter to foster discussion among your group members. Or if you prefer, you may purchase the *Best Friends Leader's Kit* from your local bookstore or through Serve International. The Leader's Kit provides all the materials necessary to conduct a 13-session course on *Best Friends*.

If you would like further details on how to start a *Best Friends* Group, you can return the enclosed Business Reply Card or write to:

Serve International
P. O. Box 723846
Atlanta, GA 30339

ABOUT THE AUTHORS

ARCHIE PARRISH is president of Serve International, an Atlanta-based training ministry that specializes in renewal, evangelism, and follow-up for church leaders and lay people. He is the author of nine previous books written under the auspices of Evangelism Explosion. He earned his B.A. degree from Southeastern Bible College, Birmingham, Alabama; his M.Div. degree from Gordon-Conwell Theological Seminary, South Hamilton, Massachusetts; and his D.Min. degree from Fuller Theological Seminary, School of Theology, Pasadena, California.

JOHN PARRISH is director of leadership training at Serve International. He received his B.A. degree from Covenant College, Lookout Mountain, Tennessee, and his M.Div. from Gordon-Conwell Theological Seminary.